Beyond the Here & Now

Thriving in the Age of Change

WHAT PEOPLE ARE SAYING ABOUT

BEYOND THE HERE & NOW

There are few books that truly explore the current human condition with such insight, passion and intelligence. Though the author does not shy away from pointing out the error of our ways, we can forgive ourselves, learn and move on to contemplate a higher purpose for ourselves that respectfully tips its hat to the great wisdoms of our ancient ancestors and embraces the incredible gifts and talents of the budding generations under our wing. Take advice from this book and our future is bright indeed.
Barbara Meiklejohn-Free, shaman and author of *The Heart of All Knowing* (O-Books) and *The Shaman Within*... (Balboa Press, Hay House (US))

This book is like a colorful, contemporary history lesson of the human spirit. It challenges us to explore what lies beyond our now failing systems and institutions which are inherently self-serving, to find what we are really capable of as a force for the good of all.
Susie Anthony, author of *A Map To God* (O-Books) and founder of The Super Hero Code

In order for a person to truly 'heal', one has to learn all one can from past experiences and embrace challenging situations. *Beyond the Here & Now* does just that on a global scale, by highlighting where we have been, where we are now, and explores the possibilities of our tomorrows. This book flies in the face of the usual 'doom and gloom' and makes a credible case for humanity's place on this living Earth.
Gaetano Vivo, Reiki Master and author of *Messages from the Angels of Transparency* (Axis Mundi Books)

Well written, researched and thought out, *Beyond the Here & Now* addresses our desire for control, deals with the real issues behind it allowing our true needs as spiritual beings to finally come to the fore.
Joylina Goodings, speaker and author of *Your Angel Journey* (O-Books)

An intelligent and enjoyable read that is brave, inspiring and ultimately uplifting...
Kate Osborne, writer/editor and founder of *Solarus Ltd.*

Beyond the Here & Now

Thriving in the Age of Change

Lucy O'Hagan

BOOKS

Winchester, UK
Washington, USA

First published by O-Books, 2013
O-Books is an imprint of John Hunt Publishing Ltd., Laurel House, Station Approach,
Alresford, Hants, SO24 9JH, UK
office1@jhpbooks.net
www.johnhuntpublishing.com

For distributor details and how to order please visit the 'Ordering' section on our website.

Text copyright: Lucy O'Hagan 2013

ISBN: 978 1 78279 154 6

A CIP catalogue record for this book is available from the British Library.

Design: Lee Nash
Cover image: Kate Osborne

Printed and bound by CPI Group (UK) Ltd, Croydon, CR0 4YY

We operate a distinctive and ethical publishing philosophy in all
areas of our business, from our global network of authors to
production and worldwide distribution.

CONTENTS

To my Family:
My parents Frank and Mary O'Hagan
Sisters Celia, Rosie, Patsy, Tina, Mary
Brothers Francis and Matt
who have been my companions, teachers and friends on this journey
through life.

Introduction

The planet Earth on which we all live and are privileged to call 'home' has, since its formation, been in a constant state of evolution. The geological structure of the Earth has changed dramatically over the millennia. Shifts in the tectonic plates which support the landmasses have on the one hand created complete mountain ranges, while at the same time causing others to submerge under rising sea levels. Rivers have emerged from these landforms cutting paths through the landscape and then, without any apparent reason or warning, have changed course or disappeared altogether.

These geological shifts and changes have been supported and often initiated by climatic conditions which, through their sheer force and power, have molded the Earth into the physical form we see today. And all are following an invisible, inaudible rhythm which is the blueprint of the Earth's evolution and journey through the Universe, being guided by the gentle hand of their Creator – a Divine Creative Force (DCF).

Where Earth has led, Nature has followed and biological life forms have reflected all these cycles, directly influenced by the ever-changing climatic and geological environment. They too have undergone constant change and adaption, from the Jurassic Era when dinosaurs roamed the Earth to its present-day inhabitants of which we Human Beings are its most complex life form. So we should not be too surprised that Earth is undergoing yet another transformation and that everyone and every living thing on this planet at this particular period of time is being affected by it.

While most plant and other life forms will automatically adapt to the changing environmental conditions as they occur and in doing so either ensure their survival or herald their extinction, humankind is in a different position. The individual is imbued with gifts that allow them to play an integral role in determining not only their future but directly influencing the course and direction of the Earth's ascension/evolution. The greatest of these gifts are the free will to choose thoughts, words, actions, and the capacity to feel emotion. These two abilities, when properly harnessed and directed, allow the individual to be a co-creator of not only their own immediate environment, but when working as part of a 'collective' with other like-minded individuals to influence change on a more global level.

This is indeed an awesome task and responsibility of which many humans are totally unaware. They are oblivious to the potential that dwells within to make this a reality and fail to recognize that just as their thoughts, words and actions can create a world of peace and abundance, misuse of these gifts can cause equal devastation.

Life, as it currently exists on Earth, has for many been about survival. We have looked to others to create our reality and to take responsibility for our personal health, education, financial well-being, moral development and safety. In fact we have been actively encouraged to place our trust in such 'experts' but as recent events have proved they are as vulnerable in the face of the Earth's current evolution as we are on an individual level. The institutions that have traditionally provided guidance and reassurance in times of crisis such as in the areas of religion, banking and the various governmental departments are themselves fighting for their very survival, as evidence of their corruption, ineptitude, gross mismanagement and wrongdoing is poured into the public arena. The banking scandals which heralded the global recession coupled with the various political and religious scandals in many countries have caused people to question if these "experts" have society's or their own best interests at heart.

Many have become disillusioned and have lost trust in the so-called 'authorities'. They are waking up to the fact that things need to change, and the way we live life here on Earth has to be rethought if we are to survive both as individuals and as a species. We can no longer look to outside establishments to provide us with the life that we wish to have, and must take responsibility for how we live our lives and begin to shape and create a world in which all can live. This includes not only humankind but all other living and sentient beings from the smallest organism to the largest. Humankind needs to become aware that, while we have an important role in the future direction of the Universe, we are directly connected to all living things and that their fate is directly linked to our own, which will impact on how we will experience life on Earth in the future.

This can be a frightening prospect for many people who feel ill-equipped to make decisions and 'create' in an environment where it seems all our sureties are being eroded. And it will necessitate replacing a lot of the values and attitudes that we currently live our life by with beliefs that allow us to move through our existing perception of limitation and helplessness. This will help release us from behaviors that are harmful not only to ourselves but to the planet on which we live. The desire for change is not of itself sufficient to 'create'; it really is only the first step along what can be a challenging road that involves self-awareness, courage, faith and honesty with the self.

This book aims to help in that process by identifying the gap that exists between our current belief systems which have limited every aspect of our lives, and those we need to adopt if we are truly to become masters of our destiny and to be the co-creators that we truly are. It will give an overview on what is happening on Earth at this time, and how we can best engage in it to assure not only our own survival but that of the planet. It will examine how each individual human has within them all the tools they need to successfully create the lives they wish to live, and how education, location, gender or age are no barriers in that journey. And it will explore the vital role that thoughts, emotions and beliefs play in that process, and suggest exercises that can help facilitate these changes to create an environment where thoughts and ideas can be actualized into our physical realities.

In order to do this we need to examine how the latest scientific research coupled with known philosophies are being dovetailed and expanded to create a new understanding of our place in the Universe and how we function within it. There are many new concepts and ideas to be incorporated which will challenge long-held beliefs and truths. The concept of 'Vibrational Energy' holds the key to our current imprisoned view of existence. This has become a term that is being widely used in a variety of contexts, and which has acquired a variety of meanings depending on the situation in which it occurs. Its use has led to a certain amount of confusion among the general public, not to mention among the various experts who believe that they are all talking about the same thing when in actuality it may be different aspects of the same topic.

It is now widely accepted by both the scientific and non-scientific communities that all living things and indeed objects oscillate at specific frequencies, which help us define the individuality of that particular item. Thanks to advancements in the area of quantum physics, this can now be objectively measured and verified. It has been further found that not only do we and the objects around us oscillate at specific frequencies, but thoughts and words also emit a vibrational frequency which scientists have only recently begun to measure. They have further discovered that the various emotional states of anger, joy, sadness have their own individual 'signature frequency' (a specific readily identifiable measurable frequency pattern) and that these signature frequencies can not only alter the overall vibrational frequency pattern of the individual form from whom they emit, but they can also affect those in the immediate environment changing their vibrational frequency pattern as well. This means that not only do we have an effect on our environment, our environment also has a direct effect on our vibrational field.

Modern-day biologists have also entered the arena to further corroborate these findings by demonstrating that the very cells of which all living things are composed actually react to external environmental stimuli as opposed to the previous theory, which postulated that cellular change occurred as a direct result of internal stimuli. The importance of this finding is that it shows us how our whole physical being is affected by the environment in which we find ourselves, by other individuals in that environment, and by the thoughts and emotional states that we create. We are also part of a planet and Universe, which itself is composed of vibrational fields. These fields not only affect us but are composed of the same basic materials (albeit packaged in different forms) as we are. Thus we are much more connected to everything in the Universe than was first suggested.

And now is the time when the Earth moves to the next step in its evolutionary journey, and all sentient beings currently residing on the planet are being given the opportunity to share in that process as a means of accelerating their own spiritual growth. Many souls have chosen to incarnate on Earth at this particular time to experience this phenomenon. This period of time has been alluded to over many centuries by many cultures, and viewed from many perspectives.

Astrologers have identified certain planetary alignments which they believe parallel major changes in human devel-opment relating to the culture, society and political structures operating at that time. These astrological ages which are particular periods of time in the astrological history of the Earth are said to signal the ending of a particular stage of life on Earth and herald the beginning of a new era where all aspects of life on Earth change. These 'ages' have been recorded by astrologers along the various centuries and in cultures as varied as the Egyptians, Mayans and Aztecs. From an astrological point of view we are between two ages the Age of Pisces, which has ended and are moving toward the Age of Aquarius. In this momentous shift there is a period of overlap, a period when we exist on the cusp between these two Ages; this period which began in 1978 will last for approximately 25 years terminating in 2012, although there remains much debate as to the exact date.

In that interim period many things will be decided, not least the future of humankind and Earth. There are many great changes occurring that depend on the interpretations and actions of others both on the Earth plane and at a galactic level. The interchange between eras is fraught with difficulties, complications and possible disasters before all is finally completed on the 21/12/12, when we will see how all has turned out as and how 'the land lies'. The outcome is by no means assured, and there is much room left for the creativity of others to help shape the structure of this brave new world.

At present the Earth is partially covered by a shadow, hidden to the most powerful of telescopes, but it is a shadow of energy that is interfering with the creative energy, some call 'love', that is being constantly transmitted from the Divine Creative Force, some call 'God' or 'Creator'. This interference has increased the sense of isolation and aloneness felt by many humans on Earth, and this has contributed greatly to the oppression, violence, despair and anger experienced by many on Earth at this time. Scientists have now become aware of this energy matrix and its effect on the physical aspects of the Earth, but are unaware of its impact on the mental and emotional well-being of every human inhabitant on Earth at this time.

Be it astrological, energetic or environmental, it is evident that there exists on Earth an imbalance. If humankind does not redress this imbalance then Mother Nature will, with severe consequences for all who stand in her path. For all our advances in science we have not as yet found a way to stop a volcano erupting, an Earth plate moving, a tsunami occurring or a hurricane forming; all that can be done are warnings issued and clear ups undertaken after the event. The scale of change is cosmic, extending far beyond the Earth, and involves many galaxies and universes and indeed (a new term that will begin to come into the Earth's vocabulary) 'hyper hectare space' is being affected by what happens. That said this is not a time for despair; rather it is a time to become co-creators in the matrix of energy that makes up the Universe. It is now imperative that those trailblazers or lightworkers incarnate now, awaken and are aware of their role, why they have come, what their contribution is to be and why so many made the journey at this juncture to be present during this time of profound change.

Their role is very simply to awaken others to what is happening and to the creative power that lies within each and every person. As more people become aware and take responsibility for their lives and actively co-create the lives that they wish to have, a critical mass is reached and humankind can create a world where many of the polarities we now experience of rich-poor, health-sickness etc. are eroded and a world is created where all can experience the abundance of the Universe. A planet where all have enough to eat, where famine, war, and destruction of resources do not exist, where humankind recognizes the connection to all things and understands our position in the Universe. Only then will we become fully aware of our true nature and our important role in the Universe.

This book seeks to give you an understanding of the building blocks that are present in the process of co-creation in the hope that by being aware of them you may choose to use them in a more effective way to create a life which fulfills all your needs, rather than one which you are forced to endure... this is your time to move beyond the here and now – it is your time to shine.

Part I

Separation from the Source

For millennia we have been actively encouraged to see and believe ourselves as separate from everything. We were encouraged to think of ourselves as masters of the Earth; above all life forms on the planet. We sought to control nature, become masters of the sky and eventually conquer space. The space race of the 60s and subsequent moon landing in 1964 all gave rise to the theory that there was nothing or nowhere that man, given enough time, would not conquer and dominate. Greater space missions were planned as humankind sought to push his sphere of influence even wider venturing on exploration missions as far afield as the planets Mars and Venus. Humankind had deemed this Universe to be his playground and had crowned himself as the most intelligent species inhabiting it.

How it came to be here was a source of much speculation and has resulted in many theories on its origin including 'a series of chemical coincidences that resulted in the 'Big Bang' from which developed matter and all subsequent life evolved' to an Infinite Intelligence which created the entire Universe and controls all movements, developments and being within this space. There are those who believe that this intelligence is ambivalent, regulating, controlling and creating as desired; while others choose to imbue it with more humanistic characteristics and believe that we humans are fashioned in its image and that it takes a personal interest in our progress, saving us when necessary, admonishing at other times or rewarding appropriate beliefs and behaviors.

The truth of the situation has yet to be conclusively proven yet within us all there is a realization that we did not arrive by accident, that there is a greater hand at work and that we as a species are a result of that handiwork. We also are painfully aware that we have become separated from the source of our creation, and this separation from Source has deprived us of an understanding of our true Nature and Being.

The historical records of humanity's progression through the ages paint a picture of a species often out of tune with its environment, other species and, on many occasions, fellow humans. This, it is postulated, is related to our biological evolution over the millennia which saw the brain evolve from the basic 'reptilian' brain, whose main focus was the survival of the species, where responses were automatic and instinctive and the ethos that 'might is right' ruled. This matured into the 'mammalian' brain with the development of the autonomic nervous system and hypothalamus, which resulted in the automatic control of body functions such as digestion, blood pressure, body temperature. The evolvement of the hippocampus allowed the instantaneous storing and filing of new experiences into a library of experience-based memories to be accessed at any time.

All of these stages contributed to the emergence of individuals who were more consciously aware of themselves in relation to their environment, and had developed feelings of anger, fear, care and the associated patterns of behavioral responses of affection, fight, flight and care of the young. Then the later development of the human specific 'neo mammalian' brain or 'thinking brain' approximately 150,000 years ago, with its capacity for language, visualization and symbolic thought, was the final aspect of brain functioning to evolve. These three distinct aspects of the brain currently operate simultaneously and are useful descriptors to explain scientifically the evolution of the functioning of the brain and the emergence of consciousness from a biological perspective.

However, that is only one aspect of the human condition; as evolution continued and humankind began to delineate between the conscious mind and the subconscious mind there was a clear separation between the roles of these two aspects of mind. While the conscious mind was focusing on reacting to stimuli encountered within its environment, the subconscious mind developed awareness on a more subtle level to ensure survival. It began to store information around the beliefs held within the community to which the individual belonged. It registered emotions and symbols. It stored all experiences and compared current situations to past events in order to make decisions and take action.

It reacted to situations and evoked emotions that were often based in fear and the need for survival. Over time it began to predict and it was this ability to predict that ensured the survival of the species, but with that devotion to predictability came a resistance to change. Change requires a response as opposed to a reaction, and as the main goal of the subconscious mind is preservation at any cost it rarely evaluates its responses, and enters into survival mode often overreacting in situations where either no action is necessary or a gentler response required. This modus operandi would have continued to be totally appropriate had we not entered a new era, one characteristic of which is the unpredictability of events, and the number of changes that are occurring at any given time.

The end of this 26,000 year cycle has been predicted over many eons by many ancient civilizations; and while there have been a variety of predictions as to how this era will both end and the new one begin, there is once again no agreement as to how this will impact on our daily lives and living. Modern science, however, now concurs that we are witnessing a planetary alignment that has not occurred for the last 26,000 years.

Many things are happening in 'linear time' that the subconscious mind does not understand, as it can only base its decisions on previous experiences. As all sureties and certainties are removed, the ability of prediction is less accurate and that has caused the subconscious mind to react with fear and anxiety as its road map proves woefully inadequate for the situations it is encountering. On a very personal level, many people predicted that they would have a meaningful relationship, perhaps marry at a certain age, have a family, be in constant employment possibly in the same job, and on the basis of that prediction they would buy a home, a car, have holidays.

Now many are finding that their job has gone (if they ever had one), that their relationship may have broken down or may not be as fulfilling as they thought, never mind other dramatic events that have challenged their belief system. In short their life has not turned out the way that they imagined, and many have no idea how to repair the situation as there are too many variables to predict with any degree of reliability. What is obvious to most is that their current way of thinking and operating in the world is not working and a new approach is needed, one that reconnects everyone with everything so that they can be more in tune with both the environment and their fellow human.

This will involve change, something that humankind finds difficult because of our need for control. To accept change is to relinquish control and enter the unknown to be at the mercy of circumstance and possibly others, to be vulnerable. And in our modern world vulnerability is regarded as weakness, and is not recognized for the strength that it truly is. In allowing ourselves to be vulnerable we open ourselves to receiving from everyone and everything including the Universe. We allow ourselves to be contributed to, to be nourished, nurtured and provided for; and this is something we have long been told that both will not occur and is not desirable.

We have been led to believe that it is best not to place ourselves in this situation for after all, as all good Darwinians will explain, life on Earth is about survival of the fittest, not contribution to those willing to receive. It is pointed out that this is the modus operandi within Nature, and it is why there are those species that are predators and those that are the prey; the predators being the strong and the prey being the weak. While on the surface this may indeed appear to be true, it does not take into account the symbiotic relationship that exists within Nature which, when left uninterrupted by outside influences, creates an environment of perfect harmony and natural order. Any attempts humankind has made to control or interfere in this natural order by introducing foreign species of animal and plant either by design or by accident has always been to the detriment of the local ecology system. The introduction of rabbits into Australia from England by Sir Thomas Austin in 1859, so that he could hunt for pleasure as he had done at home, resulted in the rabbit becoming the number one pest in Australia, doing untold damage to land and crops.

It is humankind's loss of connection with the environment as well as the sense of their own divinity that has caused them to act in isolation, oblivious to the effect that their actions are having not only on themselves but also on their environment. In this time that sense of connectedness and oneness with all things is reemerging to be reestablished as the basic premise of life here on Earth.

Part 2

Preparation

Humankind has been preparing for this change for some time, although not consciously aware of it. In every generation there have been a number of individuals who have incarnated on this Earth with the prime objective of guiding human beings forward along a particular path in our evolution. Individuals such as Abraham Lincoln, who in the 1800s abolished slavery in North America and moved humankind from the viewpoint that it was acceptable to 'own' another human being, to take away their rights, dignity and freedom based on the color of their skin, to a new perspective that viewed all men of every color as equal. He rededicated his country to the notion of liberty, equality and freedom for all its citizens.

Likewise in India, Mahatma Gandhi in the 1900s helped secure the freedom of his country and people from colonial rule by introducing the idea of "resistance against tyranny through nonviolence." He very ably demonstrated that by harnessing the minds and hearts of the masses in a program of non-cooperation much could be achieved along the road of personal and national freedom. This idea of 'people power' and 'peaceful revolution' became the blueprint for the Civil Rights movement right across the world and still operates today.

In more recent times Nelson Mandela has in South Africa taken this one step further by demonstrating forgiveness of his oppressors and captors. He along with others such as Archbishop Desmond Tutu have played a pivotal role in not only advocating but demonstrating reconciliation, forgiveness and working together for the common good to build a society where all can prosper regardless of their color, gender or beliefs.

These men and many more unsung heroes both male and

female have sought to rectify injustice, introduce new thinking or modify long-held beliefs and practices. They have been prepared to accept the consequences of going against the commonly-held view and have blazed a trail along unknown paths. Such trail-blazers have been a feature in the evolution of humankind and have led where we all now follow. They have been a constant, and have acted as guides throughout history changing the common perspective and exhorting humankind to be the best they can be.

The lead to the current change we are experiencing entered a new phase at the beginning of the 20th century when there was a shift in the energetic dynamics operating on the Earth plane and a rebalancing of the male and female energies. These energy dynamics do not correspond specifically to gender as every human regardless of their sex carries both male and female energies and can therefore be said to have qualities that reflect this. However, each gender will carry a greater percentage of the energy type that they espouse. Males will have a greater proportion of male energy than females, and the females a greater proportion of female energy than males.

The male energy is regarded as being more direct, logical and action-focused while the feminine energy is seen as being more nurturing, intuitive and passive. It is the interaction between the two that creates a balance both in the individual and on a larger scale in the society and world in which we inhabit. This concept of duality is not new and has been around for many millennia. Ancient Chinese philosophy, from as far back as 2000 BC, openly discussed the notion that all living things contain energy that is opposite in nature. They believed that the Universe began with 'Qi' (Life Force/Energy) and through its movement and variation two poles were created, 'Yin' and 'Yang', and as all things in the Universe are produced by movement and variation in Qi so everything can be divided into aspects of Yin and Yang e.g. heaven/Earth, night/day etc.

Yin and Yang are opposites and because of this opposition they are interactive which causes movement and hence change. This opposition is not absolute, in that within Yang there are seeds of Yin and vice versa, nor is it 50/50; rather it is a dynamic and constantly changing balance. They are also interdependent for 'solitary Yang cannot exist and solitary Yin cannot grow'. The Yang energy which is regarded as being more masculine in nature is dynamic, fiery and active while the Yin energy which is more feminine is passive, dark and nurturing. It is the combination and interaction of the two that create life, and when that balance becomes disturbed in that one becomes more dominant, then disharmony, discord and ultimately 'dis–ease' result.

Prior to the 1900s the male energy was the more dominant energy on the planet and thus the society of the day reflected this. There was much more emphasis on action which when put to good use translated into new inventions and discoveries that benefited all humankind. The invention of steel, petroleum and electricity in the 19th century heralded the Industrial Revolution which formed the foundations of many of the lifestyle products that we take for granted today. But it also resulted in a disconnection between many human beings and the land. Large numbers of people moved from the country into urban areas to be nearer the great factories that provided employment, and in doing so severed their direct link with Nature and the feminine energies that such a relationship offered.

Over successive generations this bond became successively weaker, and the land and nature came to be viewed by many as a resource that could be used to provide the raw materials for the industries that had been developed and was there for the taking. It was into this background that the first wave of rebalancing energy arrived and signaled the reemergence of the 'Divine Feminine', an energy that was feminine in the qualities that it imbued the Earth with and reminded all of the nurturing, caring, nourishing aspects necessary to create a caring environment for all.

It was around this time that women in New Zealand secured the right to vote. This was followed in England and soon became a worldwide phenomenon. This was indeed a landmark occurrence as until then women had been regarded as an extension of the dominant male in their lives and had little rights or power. This was the first time that all women irrespective of their age, status, class or education were given a chance to move forward and begin to think of themselves as something other than an object to be controlled by males; their opinion, their 'vote' counted.

The two world wars served to reduce the stronghold that the patriarchal society had on females. It was during these years that the divine feminine continued to steadily emerge to counteract the masculine principle, which hitherto insisted that the only way to resolve differences was through conflict. This belief culminated in wars, which resulted in the mass removal of souls from the planet. In the Second World War economic conditions in Europe and the Americas necessitated that women leave the home to work in positions and locations that previously would not have been permitted by their families. This gave women a taste of what it was like to earn their own money, make their own decisions and indeed mistakes, and what was more it was done with the tacit approval if not insistence of the establishment. The 'genie was out of the bottle' and could not be put back in.

When the war was over it was impossible for things to return to how they were. People were changed. For men the horrors of war had left their mark and many were physically, mentally and emotionally scarred by their experiences. For women a new sense of worth had been discovered; they had been their own mistresses and had opinions and ideas that would no longer be silenced. A new 'normality' had to be found to accommodate both sets of experiences and beliefs. The experience of war made an indelible impression on both sexes in those generations directly affected, and reinforced the idea that mass violence and hatred was not the way forward.

The use of radio and television made the Second World War much more real for many not directly involved in fighting. It allowed people on a worldwide basis to see, hear and bear witness to the brutality of war in a way that no other form of media had ever done previously, and in doing so caused many to question the legitimacy of conflict as a means of settling international disputes and gaining national objectives.

In the 1940s and 1950s much time was spent on reestablishing the nuclear family as the central plank in society. There was a heartfelt desire for a social order and a sense of stability that had been missing in the previous decades. People needed to feel in control of their lives and yearned for a 'normality' that belied the chaos of the previous era. However, the overregulation and distrust that occurs in a security aware country at war had become enshrined in the bureaucracy of its institutions and this continued, causing many to resent this state intrusion and control of many aspects of their private lives.

It was not long before the rules and regulations of this period were being challenged by the younger members of society who had had a less direct experience of the chaos of war. There was a cry for more free expression, and changes emerged tentatively at first in the areas of music, dance, dress codes: the era of rock and roll had arrived. By the 1960s the idea that society needed to change to allow more personal and societal freedom for all not just the chosen few was being voiced. And once again there were bands of trailblazers who stepped forward to lead the way and who were willing to risk their own liberty and often life in the pursuit of equality for all; to ensure change in all areas of life here on Earth including civil rights, the arts, music, literature, medicine, and economics all needed to be challenged and to evolve.

In America this process was instigated by Mrs. Rosa Parks

who refused to give up her seat and move to the back of a bus because she was black and forbidden by segregation laws to sit in the white section of the bus. Her action and the subsequent reaction of the local authorities sparked an indignation that led to the Civil Rights movement emerging to demand removal of these divisive laws. This movement was led by Dr. Martin Luther King who eventually succeeded in having segregation repealed in the United States of America, but who paid the ultimate price with his life. Dr. King's example inspired people all over the world to join together to fight injustice in a peaceful manner They were often met with force from the authorities and many of these protests became mini battlefields with casualties on both sides.

In the cultural world of the Arts, battles were also occurring although much less bloody. The boundaries were being pushed as to what constituted Art, Literature and Music. This was a reaction to the overregulated 50s when censorship, repression, familial and societal duty were not so much expected as demanded. There was a much greater push towards free expression, and 'pop art' became in vogue with Andy Warhol being one of its 'leading lights'. Art was being redefined, as to what constituted art and what constituted 'good art'.

On the music front 'pop music' erupted on to the scene with the Beatles creating a new 'beat' which captured the imagination of the youth in both Europe and the USA, and eventually becoming a worldwide phenomenon. In literature many authors grasped topics that were previously taboo and revealed the darker sides of humanity while others described the rugged realities of life as a member of a particular ethnic or minority group. In America James Baldwin explored the difficulties of being a member of two minority groups being homosexual and black in his book *Go Tell It on the Mountain*, while Ken Kesey wrote about his experiences working in a psychiatric ward and as a volunteer in government experiments with LSD and other drugs in *One Flew Over the Cuckoo's Nest*. Many of these new art forms were banned as being harmful to the moral values of the age and often these attempts at censorship only fuelled the desire and debate for change.

Religious institutions were also undergoing change. In the Roman Catholic Church the occasion of Vatican II produced a document that essentially overhauled many of the more outdated doctrines of the Church to embrace viewpoints which allowed for a gentler, more benevolent God to emerge, where 'Love' not retribution and vengeance was to be the teaching and message of the Church. There was to be a greater involvement and participation of the ordinary people in the administrative and ceremonial aspects of church life. Many other religions were undergoing huge changes; with the Chinese invasion of Tibet many Buddhist monks and nuns were forced into exile all over the world often with only their beliefs, teachings and practices as luggage. They brought these teachings to the West and so intro-duced new concepts and ways of thinking which had not been encountered before.

There was political upheaval on a worldwide scale in many continents. Huge numbers of people were displaced and became refugees and many with the advent of war moved from the East to the West bringing with them their culture, knowledge, spiritual and religious practices, new ways of thinking, differing beliefs and attitudes, all of which were added to the melting pot of change.

This was more the adolescence of the Divine Feminine, when much potential was spotted but no one had any real idea of how to make it work. Excesses were the norm and while many started off with pure aims and intentions they really had no idea how to control, guide or direct this newfound energy which was having such a direct impact on all aspects of human creativity and thinking, instigating change in all aspects of daily life.

One of the first taboos to fall victim to the new wave of thinking was the whole area of sexuality, which up until then had been seriously repressed, censored and controlled. It had been deemed the sole province of the married couple for the purpose of propagation of the species, and homosexuality was a criminal offence for which there were harsh custodial sentences. It was not talked about but shrouded in secrecy, and there were severe societal consequences for those who engaged in any form of sexual intimacy outside marriage, although it was usually the female who bore the social stigma of having an illegitimate child. The introduction of the contraceptive pill and the ready availability of condoms allowed a new sexual freedom that had never been experienced by any generation before. Gone was the fear of pregnancy and social retribution; in its place was an opportunity to explore a part of the self that had been forbidden and frowned upon.

When used in its purest form as a physical expression of love, commitment and trust, sexual energy can strengthen the love and connection already existing between two individuals, and bring their relationship to a higher level. This concept is very much part of many Eastern philosophies and part of the teaching in many indigenous cultures. In India the use of sexual energy as a means of reaching spiritual enlightenment is encapsulated in a series of teachings known as 'tantra'. It is a complete branch of spiritual philosophy in its own right. Similarly in the Taoism traditions of Eastern Asia the ability of sexual union to alter states of being and lead the couple to a deeper more fulfilling relationship that will ultimately strengthen the bonds of love between them is also emphasized. This not only builds the relationship between the couple, but its effect is felt throughout the whole community as it increases stability, respect and love.

In the West during the 1960s the 'sexual revolution' became as much hedonistic as it was spiritual, as very few had the knowledge necessary to direct it onto a meaningful pathway. At this point we are not talking exclusively about 'free love'; that was part of it but a greater, more potent part of the energy was to see each other as 'brothers', as being of one divine family, not separate from and distrustful of each other. It gave people the idea (which had long been forgotten) that we were all responsible for each other, that we all had a duty of care to those less able, less wealthy, less healthy, less free. There was a new awareness that the world was a concern to us all, not just a few people in places of power, and highlighted the fact that we all were citizens of the world and that by banding together we could effect change and so 'cosmic consciousness' was reborn.

This principle, while 'new' to the baby boomers of the 1960s, had indeed been present in the indigenous peoples of the world who for eons had lived by this code. The Aborigines in Australia, the Maori in New Zealand, the Dogon in Africa, the Natives of the Americas – all the ancient peoples and tribes viewed themselves as part of the Cosmos and had a sense of their place in the Cosmos. They were its children and it was their home but modern man had lost that connection, seeing himself as separate from his environment and indeed master of it as opposed to part of it. The Divine Feminine awakened what essentially is a fundamental knowing in all of us that we are part of something much greater than just the community or planet we live in.

Many tried to expand their consciousness into the Cosmos by the use of mind-expanding drugs, but once again their lack of knowledge about astral travel and control of the mind meant that these excursions into various other dimensions were very much a hit and miss affair diluted down to 'good trip' versus 'bad trip'. No one had any idea what they were dealing with nor had they a road map to help guide them, so there were many casualties, those who succumbed to addiction, overdoses or damaged their mental processes and sense of reality permanently.

The Divine Feminine energy was, however, anchored and it did take root and has continued to grow and blossom ever since. In the 1970s there was a setback to such ideals with the onset of the AIDS epidemic. The sexual energy which had exploded with such force had to find a new balance, one which was less destructive. There was a need to restore the spiritual aspect of sexual energy. It had become for many people an act of lust, exploitation and pure animal instinct. There was no focus on the exchange of energy between the two individuals; it was only a moment of pleasure. In this way its potency and sacredness became diminished as it was indulged in with a variety of partners and no thought or care given to those involved. This period had become synonymous with excess in all its shapes and forms.

It became obvious with those that had eyes to see that a new balance needed to be found, and that all people needed to reevaluate the way that they were living their lives. The use of alcohol and drugs had reached epidemic proportions among certain groups and the effects of addiction to both these substances were on the rise globally with social order being threatened. Equilibrium needed to be restored in order to prevent humanity from destroying itself, and the AIDS epidemic was the catalyst that began the process. Its origins are unknown and theories vary widely as to when, where and how it emerged but its effects were quickly felt. It cast a long shadow over all the communities in which it appeared, causing fear and panic. People became distrustful and fearful of one another; for some that fear turned to hatred and rage as many looked for someone or some group to blame for this turn of events.

The 1980s saw the effects of the AIDS epidemic spread wider throughout communities across all ages, genders and social groupings. People had long forgotten about the concept of cosmic consciousness, and were more concerned about their own survival and meeting their own material needs. This culture of materialistic self-gratification grew and the connection between humans and Mother Earth was further severed as humankind truly began to see the Earth as an object devoid of any life-giving qualities, to be used and abused as he wished. The age of consumerism had truly arrived in the West now that there was no fear of food shortages, and basic survival was assured.

There was another threat in the 1980s that threatened the future of the world and that was nuclear war. Quietly and in the backgrounds the major superpowers had been developing nuclear weapons since end of the Second World War as a means of assuring their supremacy. The deadliness of these weapons had been very ably demonstrated at Hiroshima and Nagasaki in Japan on the 6th and 9th August 1945 when America dropped an atomic bomb in each of these cities killing approximately 80–100,000 in Hiroshima, and 60–80,000 in Nagasaki with roughly 50% dying on the first days. Nuclear weapons, they assured the public, were being developed purely to act as deterrents against threats from hostile countries but as in all things empty threats and posturing very quickly became a more menacing reality as the arms race began in earnest with both sides vying for domination.

The world separated along the East-West divide as 'The Cold War' became a game of brinkmanship and subterfuge. People became afraid with each viewing the other side as the enemy, and countries who once were allies found themselves on opposite sides of the nuclear argument. Choices had to be made and these choices often boiled down to continued economic links versus moral beliefs, with many countries choosing the former to ensure their economic survival in the recession that was occurring. Once again there were those individuals who were determined to take a stand and mobilize others to call for worldwide nuclear disarmament; their calls were not welcomed and they were viewed by authorities and many individuals alike as a threat to national security and unpatriotic. Their view for a world free of nuclear armaments was deemed unrealistic and fantastical, out of step with the reality that existed; but nevertheless they persisted and in doing so widened the debate around the moral values and direction that we as a global race wished to espouse.

They may not have succeeded in their ultimate goal of having a world free of nuclear arms. In fact at present there are now many more countries with nuclear facilities than at any other time; but what they did do was bring it from the shadows and place it center stage so that all could be aware of what was taking place. By shining the light on nuclear armament they changed the course of its implementation and challenged its legitimacy as a valid means of warfare. They also informed the public at large about the dangers of nuclear energy both to themselves and their environment so that it could no longer be regarded as just the next step in weaponry development.

By the end of the 1980s there was a revival in the world's economy, partly driven by the expansion in the defense industries, and suddenly all souls became fascinated with the idea of ownership. All manner of baubles were dangled in front of humans in the Western world as 'must haves'; once people began to buy into that idea, it was very easy to manipulate them into believing that what they 'must have' was good for them. Ugliness replaced beauty in many creative fields; natural order and harmony whether in music, art, or literature was replaced by discordance and disharmony. In music the use of electronically-generated sound to create replaced for many composers the use of instruments, with dissonance and volume the order of the day. Lyrics became more violent, aggressive and explicit. This was deemed to be of the moment, and any concern voiced was dismissed as an attempt to curb creativity. In the Art world conceptual art became popular which featured among its most celebrated award-winning works dead animals preserved in formaldehyde.

Computer games and computer-generated images became the toys of choice for many young people, and the ever-increasing violence of the games being played soon came to be accepted as the norm. All of these forms of 'entertainment' affected the human subconscious, but because people had now lost their sense of discernment they could not see or feel the damage that such creations were doing to their sense of well-being and harmony, and they further reduced their connection and appreciation of beauty and the natural order. The expansion of the World Wide Web while giving instant access to information on a global level had birthed a new way of communicating between people; social networking sites were launched that allowed individuals to 'meet' without ever leaving their computer screens. Friendships became 'virtual' and for some what was happening online became equally or more important than what was occurring in their daily lives.

By the mid 1990s many individuals had so lost their sense of belonging they began to look for some way of feeling 'real', of reconnecting. Particularly the youth who had had their formative years shaped by a culture which set out to 'shock' the senses through constant dissonance, violence and discord. Their 'salvation' came in the form of drugs, cocaine, heroin, alcohol, all of which numbed their pain and temporarily stopped the feelings of isolation and loss. Like their predecessors in the 60s many succumbed to the lifestyle that addiction eventually leads to, and whole communities were devastated and trapped into a spiral of despair.

In the Western world there were food surpluses caused by common agricultural policies that sought to reward those who produced most without any respect for the natural rhythm of the land. Advances in science ensured that both land and animals produced greater yields as farming became yet more 'intensive' with very little thought being given to the overall welfare of either the land or the animals involved. Many people were becoming obese with all the food that was being produced and eaten. Methods of food production changed and, little by little, more and more chemicals were being introduced into the food chain, so more and more the connection between the life-giving force of nature as witnessed by the food she produces was being reduced. By now the masses were at the control of the producers and advertisers, so it was easy to convince them that this food was good for them, that processed food was the way forward and that their lack of discernment meant that all this was accepted with no difficulty.

In the meantime the AIDS epidemic continued to spread and its influence began to be felt in Africa, the Far East and SE Asia. War, famine and sickness ran rife through Africa, removing many souls from the Earth plane and sewing despair and illness where once there had been life and hope. The isolation of the individual engendered feelings of helplessness in all those who viewed the scene. Once again there were a few strong individuals who banded together to begin to fight back and blaze a trail from helplessness into action. They no longer accepted the view that there was nothing anyone could do in such circumstances, that all were powerless to help.

The whole Live Aid movement began with one individual, Sir Bob Geldof, deciding that something had to be done to help those starving in Ethiopia and with one phone call began a force that ended up galvanizing hundreds of musicians and ancillary staff donating their talents for free in concerts worldwide, and involving millions of people around the world taking action to help those in dire need of help. Their focus was to reawaken people to their ability to help others less fortunate and once again to remind them that they could make a difference, and so cosmic consciousness reappeared. The balance shifted slightly and where once apathy reigned, little sparks of social conscience began; music and art were the catalysts that began this movement, people who had been stunned into silence or who had just come of age began to be drawn to each other. This was necessary to restore the balance on the planet as people began to feel that they as individuals could make a contribution, could have a say and help change the world in which they lived.

In the early 2000s this cosmic consciousness continued with a concentrated effort by the 'Drop the Debt' international campaign fronted by Bono the lead singer from the band U2 and Sir Bob Geldof to have more developed countries cancel the monetary debts owed to them by Third World countries. The repayments of those loans were essentially crippling the poorer countries and preventing any meaningful development within them. In March 2000, America, France, Canada, the United Kingdom and Germany among others all announced the cancelling of loans to Third World countries. At the same time the HIV/AIDS epidemic which had been running unchecked in Africa with such devastation began to be tackled in a more systematic way with the provision of antiretroviral drugs. Despite this, in 2007 92% of all HIV/AIDS-related deaths occurred in Africa. The 'noughties' also saw the concept of global warming become a mainstream topic as the Kyoto Agreement, which had been signed in 1997, became active in February 2005.

The 191 countries which had pledged to reduce their greenhouse gas emissions were now being held accountable as to the efforts that they had made to achieve this. The environment was center stage and as more ordinary people became aware of the effects of pollution on Mother Earth so the clamor grew for governments to take action in this respect. The realization that if humankind does not change his behavior and his attitude towards the environment and the planet Earth that it will no longer be able to support future generations, and that we as a species may very well have signed our own extinction warrant, was now apparent.

That work continues to this day, but with each year the sense of urgency and momentum gathers pace; more and more trailblazers join the battle to make a difference to conditions on this world for the benefit of all. Those projects, which are numerous and often very local, such as clearing litter from an area, dredging a river, recycling schemes or creating a community group to care for an area, have at their core the pure intentions of assisting Mother Nature, and humankind is having an effect on the Earth helping raise its vibrational level. Little by little things are improving, cosmic consciousness has been reestablished and begins to grow, more information is being accessed so that others may awaken and find what it is they came to do; even at the darkest there is always hope, light and life.

In schools children are being taught about our connection to the environment and how best we can look after it. The direct connection with Mother Earth is reemerging as many choose to start growing their own food and keep their own food-giving animals. People want to live sustainable lifestyles, and now there is much more research and many more products that can give us the convenience and comfort of modern living without harming or damaging the Earth. All these innovations are in their infancy, but as more individuals become aware and make choices that support Mother Earth they can change the future direction of life on the planet.

The outcome is not certain, more people are being awakened to the awareness that we are spiritual beings in a physical body, that we are one with Divine Creation and that we have been given a special gift of co-creation that we must learn to invoke and use responsibly. We must believe that we are not at the mercy of a few powerful individuals or institutions who decide how it is we are to live our lives, or that we have no control over the direction our lives are to take. Rather we need to accept that we are now at a point in the evolution of the planet and of humankind where we evolve to the next level or dimension. A level that will see humankind freed from the shackles of his own limited thinking and ready to accept the responsibility of being a co-creator.

To that end we are witnessing a time of unparalleled change when the unthinkable becomes reality and all certainty is eroded. The twin pillars of economics and monetary systems which for so long have been the cornerstone of global wealth have been broken with such rapidity and finality that most refuse to believe that they have gone. Much time, effort and resources are being poured in to try and revive them but they will not be resurrected for they have no place in the new world which is emerging. The final shape of that new world is not yet determined and will rely on the ability of humankind to develop a system which is inclusive of all and not just the chosen few. It must be fair, equitable, transparent and accessible, for nothing less will be accepted.

As in any war there are casualties: some are the most vulnerable human beings in society whose feelings of helplessness and hopelessness seduce them into believing that death is the only solution and so they take their own lives in the mistaken belief that the world is better off without them; for others addiction to drugs, toxic substances, alcohol, and starvation serve to blind them to who they really are and they travel through life asleep, oblivious to their potential and power. There are also those souls who have chosen difficult roles to experience, those living in impoverished physical circumstances, those who are vulnerable emotionally or mentally and those who by virtue of their destination on this Earth must meet all the challenges that such a location throws up.

This constant effort to remain in balance affects our physical body as what we think and feel has a direct effect on the body. The endocrine system which, with the nervous system, has responsibility for preserving and coordinating all body systems by maintaining a chemical balance throughout the body is under particular stress. It maintains balance in the body by secreting hormones from various glands and cells located throughout the body. One of the most important glands is the adrenal gland, which is situated above each kidney. It is the gland which determines the body's response to stress and as stress levels increase and occur for ever-prolonged periods it is the one gland that can malfunction and cause an autoimmune disorder. Many diseases due to autoimmune disorders are present on the Earth plane and these are set to increase as further pressures are put on the adrenal glands. In fact there are those scientists who now believe that stress is responsible for 95% of all disease in humans at present.

This is not totally surprising when we consider the old proverb 'as above so below, as without so within'. This has been the mantra of many indigenous and philosophical teachings and once again draws attention to the fact that as we are part of the Universe and of this planet, if the planet is out of balance then we as inhabitants will also reflect that imbalance. Quantum physics backs this up having found that our molecular structures are made of the same constituents that make up the Universe and environment that we live in. As our awareness and knowledge of how the Universe works develops, there will come solutions as to how the physical, mental and emotional energies can be brought into balance in each individual. Many of these disorders will disappear as people make the changes necessary to realign themselves with a Divine Creative Force.

And so we begin to look at our role in this new energetic world where everything has changed beyond recognition, where all absolutes have been removed and the ability to survive these changes are dependent on our awareness of, and use of, the tools that we have at our disposal to meet all the challenges. We at this stage in our evolution are only beginning to discover how to become well-equipped to not only meet these changes but in fact manipulate them and create a world where we all can be happy, fulfilled and at peace.

Part 3

Mind Over Heart

Although a very great deal has been written about the nature of the Human Mind, have we really come any closer to understanding it? It has been discussed from many viewpoints: philosophical, psychological, and psychiatric. All of which have offered their own ideas as to its true nature, its role in our life and how to manage it. In Vedic texts, written thousands of years ago in India, the mind was not regarded in the same way as it is today. It was seen as being part of a process that had at its center the heart. It was by tuning into the heart that decisions were made, responses gauged and the self known. The mind was an integral and important part of that process, and its role was very much to serve the heart, to carry out its wishes. Once a decision was made it was the mind's role to work out how best to carry that decision out. In this way one always acted with integrity and in a way that ensured a right course of action or response for all involved. The heart was the master, the mind its servant.

Similarly in Traditional Chinese Medicine it is the heart that is regarded as the Emperor of the body, for it is in the heart that the 'Shen' or mind resides. If the heart is disturbed then the mind has nowhere to rest, and as a result agitation, restlessness, disordered sleep patterns and mental imbalances may occur. It is interesting to note that recent scientific studies within the area of quantum physics are beginning to come to similar conclusions.

Lynn McTaggart in her book *The Field* discusses how we are essentially information systems that are accessing information from the Cosmos or 'The Field' (invisible matter) and are sending out information into that field which then creates our reality. The heart, she suggests, may be the master organ or 'Emperor' in this dynamic communication, and may be the "carry wave for information modulated with emotional pattern", which is then directed to other organs within the body via the circulation system. The rhythmic beating patterns of the heart reflect the emotional state being conveyed, and in order for the rest of the body organs to be in coherence with the brain neurons a good beating pattern is necessary. The heart receives the information first as it responds faster to environmental stimuli by virtue of the fact that there are more neural pathways running from the heart to the brain than the other way around. The heart then relays the information to the brain, which depending what picture is before it will initiate a response. Lynn McTaggart suggests the heart and brain have access to a field of information unbound by time or space.

When we talk about the 'Heart' we are not only referring to the physical organ but the 'Sacred Heart', that sacred space within each and every one of us where we are in direct commune with that aspect of ourselves known by various names – 'intuition', 'higher self', 'soul'. It is in this sacred space that we can commune in a direct and loving way with that still, quiet voice that always knows what is best for us, guiding us through this often-confusing maze of 'life'. The mind owes its allegiance to the heart; its role is to carry out its wishes in the most effective and loving way possible but at present for many this is not the case.

In our modern world for many individuals the mind has ceased to serve the heart, and has instead become the master. The psychologist Carl Jung, often regarded as the father of Modern Psychology, was one of the first to explore the aspects of mind and more particularly the relationship between the conscious and unconscious mind which he felt was more spiritual in origin. The mind can be regarded as having three separate but interdependent departments: the conscious, subconscious and superconscious.

The Conscious mind is that part which we humans are most

aware of. It deals with the day-to-day perceptions of life as seen through the five senses and sees life as it appears to be. It is regarded as analytical, masculine, yang or as defined by Carl Jung the 'animus'. The 'thinking mind' that uses deductive reasoning and using factual information from the five senses to formulate theories and judgments which it then inputs or sends to the second aspect of mind, the subconscious.

The Subconscious mind is the powerhouse or storage center for all our thoughts, ideas, beliefs and attitudes, and is the core from which all our responses emerge. It is regarded as feminine, yin or the anima of Jungian theory. It is a competent, insensitive, non-thinking computer that will serve up all that has been programmed into it. It has no powers of deduction or initiation, merely responds to requests sent to it via the conscious mind. Whatever we imagine or feel deeply about, the subconscious will carry out in the most minute detail. It does not evaluate the effects of its actions; its role is to serve. It uses 'inductive reasoning' and gives a picture of reality depending on what has been fed into it. It is where all our habits are stored and it protects itself from change by emotional rather than analytical responses. This is why we often find ourselves reacting in a habitual way to a new event because it reminds us of a previous experience and we have been triggered emotionally by our subconscious. The subconscious cannot reprogram itself; it has to be done by the individual who on reflection decides that a changed reaction would be more advantageous and changes the programming accordingly.

It also explains why an expressed desire to change a behavior that is no longer serving us is not enough, and why good intentions or stated affirmations do not result in success. Unless we identify the programming that we have in our subconscious regarding that topic or behavior and modify that programming, we will not succeed in our desire to change. This is why despite our best efforts we can often fail to implement the changes we desire. For example if I make a conscious decision that 'I want to be rich' and put all my efforts into creating money and make positive statements and affirmations 'I am rich', 'I deserve to be rich' etc., but have in my subconscious the belief that 'money brings unhappiness' or 'no one in my family ever gets rich', then regardless of the action I take my quest to create wealth will not succeed because the subconscious and the conscious are not aligned, and it is the subconscious that ultimately will create my reality based on the beliefs held there. The subconscious also is a filter between the conscious and the third aspect of mind, the superconscious. It is a bridge between the finite and the infinite.

The Superconscious Mind (referred to as the 'God Mind', 'Higher Self', Intuition, 'Qi' or 'Prana'), that part which is the most closely related to the Divine, contains the blueprint for our time on Earth. It acts as a moral and spiritual barometer for the way we live our life on Earth. This concept of a pathway or route to the Divine or other world is not new and has occurred in the belief systems of many indigenous tribes and peoples throughout the world. The shamans of the Indian tribes, the priests of Inca, Mayan and Egyptian traditions were all said to be adept at travelling in this 'other world' to bring back the wisdom stored there. When these three parts of the mind operate as a whole in dealing with life the challenges we meet within it are more easily managed.

However, for the majority of the population on Earth at this time the direct connection to the 'superconscious' aspect of the mind has not been fully developed or indeed has become dimmed due to underuse. We have stopped listening to the voice within or retreating to that heart space, and have instead created a greater reliance on the subconscious to meet our needs and make our decisions. In some instances we have stopped making decisions at all and have handed over our power to outside agencies or experts to decide what is best for us. This separation from the Source, God, the Universe, Creator (or what other name you wish to identify it by) means that a lot of our reactions and the emotions evoked are often based on fear and survival as opposed to love. As previously stated, the main goal of the subconscious mind is preservation at any cost; it rarely evaluates its responses and enters into survival mode often overreacting to situations where either no action is necessary or a gentler response required. This links back to the remnants of our 'reptilian' brain, where the desire for food, fornication, fight and flight prevailed.

In this time of change many things are occurring in 'linear time' that the subconscious mind does not understand as it can only base its decisions on previous experiences. As its sureties and certainties are removed, situations where once the mind could predict the outcome it can no longer do so. On a very personal level many people confidently predicted that they would be in constant employment for years to come and therefore could afford to buy a home, a car or whatever. They did not predict that there was a banking crisis looming which would trigger a global recession that would result in their losing their jobs and in some cases their homes, savings or cause them to be saddled with debts that they were unable to pay.

The recent natural disasters in Haiti and Japan were not predicted by our modern technologies and the scale of devastation that ensued is outside anything previously encountered or experienced by anyone, with the result that many people are overwhelmed by both the enormity of the catastrophe and the suddenness of it. The Mind is currently out of its depth and has no idea how to remedy the situation except to batten down the hatches and in some cases go into a frenzied overload of activity, reasoning that, 'If I continue to live the way I am living but just go faster, work for longer or harder, then everything will be alright.' This thinking will, however, not suffice.

Time is speeding up, and by this we mean the number and complexity of both physical situations and spiritual incidences requiring attention that are occurring in any given time period is increasing. Situations, lessons or karmic debt that may have taken lifetimes to complete are now being completed within a very short period of time. Human Beings are having to contend with more dramas, more crises, more learning situations than ever before, each year it increases tenfold and will continue to do so, so how will the mind cope if it does not change its modus operandi? Simply, it won't. It cannot keep operating at its current level or speed of functioning, because to do so will result in 'burnout' for the people involved. Those individuals who try to carry on as before will in fact discover that they cannot do so, and insistence on doing so will result in a range of mental problems depending on the level of mental rigidity and their need to control.

Some who are unable, or closed to change may have complete psychological meltdowns, shutting down completely, unable to participate in life; others will become totally terrified of the world, feeling paranoid, isolated and alone, with greater numbers suffering agoraphobia or claustrophobia, all leading to very challenging existences. However, large numbers of individuals will begin to accommodate these changes and begin to release the need for control, putting their trust in the Divine and recognizing their own position as co-creators with the Divine. They will not be at the mercy of circumstances but rather go with the flow, seeing opportunities in every situation and creating the lives that they wish to experience. This does not mean that they will not meet challenges or suffer loss; they will, but their awareness and flexibility will allow them to go within to receive clarity and access more solutions. Many who are not able to do this either through lack of awareness or lack of belief may choose not to stay on the Earth plane and so suicide will become more common.

All human beings will be feeling the stress of this increase in the time/space ratio and all will feel the effect. The body which is itself an energy matrix will register the change in which it is being asked to react to things. The endocrine system which is the chemical reactor of the body and very closely linked to the emotional body will bear the brunt of this stress and will have difficulty in maintaining balance; for many that system will fail to function adequately or will break down completely. The adrenal glands will become depleted in many individuals as they live in a constant state of stress; only those that take steps to adjust to this exceptional period of change will escape relatively lightly although not totally unscathed, for by their very nature the changes occurring are affecting all souls in human form at this time. These depleted adrenal glands will eventually affect the whole immune system which will eventually become compromised, leading to a huge upsurge in the number of autoimmune disorders, some known to the medical profession others not; debilitating symptoms which affect the quality of life but for which there is no medical cure.

Many humans over the next 5–7 years will become increasingly tired of the lives they are leading, the frenetic pace, the stress, the constant physical exhaustion. Their dissatisfaction will encourage many to make life-affirming changes and begin to listen to their hearts instead of the mind. Others will listen to the logic of the mind, which tells them there is no other way, that's how it's got to be, and it is this group who are the most vulnerable to the system breakdowns described earlier.

So what can be done at this time to cope with this period of cosmic disturbances, and maintain balance within it? The first thing is to be aware that it is happening and that we need to address the way in which we have been living our lives here on Earth. We each have a set of beliefs – attitudes and ideas that dictate our approach to life, from where we live, to the work that we do, the friends that we make and how we spend our money. These choices are influenced both directly and indirectly by the belief systems that we inherited from our family, communities, governments – any particular group that we have identified with. This is now the time to start questioning whether those beliefs and attitudes are serving us or are limiting us for they are indeed controlling our thinking and the choices we make. The basic premise of all things that seek to control is that: (a) we are not aware of the controls that exist; and (b) if we did we would seek to remove those controls.

In the first scenario it is indeed true that we are not aware of the many controls that have been placed on us. They are invariably placed by governments, religions, cultural norms and even by families and friends. The idea is if most people agree to them and carry them out then they become the norm and people stop questioning why they are doing things. Any queries can be answered by the mantra 'because that's the way it is'; after a period of time people stop questioning, forget to question or indeed assume that they have no choice because after all what can one person do against an institution?

The survival of Institutions is dependent on not being questioned or having their authority challenged. By assuring all of their integrity and competency they assuage any fears and can 'divide and conquer' quite easily. Through time they become accepted as the experts and the general population develops a sense of apathy and helplessness; in this way the populace can be easily managed. Ultimately there are only a very few people, an elite group, that wield the power and keep the masses in check. They do not need to be well armed or to knockout everyone that challenges them, only on the rare occasions when examples are needed, or precedents set. Otherwise they are quite happy to rely on the general apathy of the masses and that innate sense that human beings have to belong. This allows them to maintain some of the most draconian and barbaric forms of control with the seeming blessing of the people. This is not unique to one culture; all cultures, all nations, all sexes are being controlled. Some in different ways to others, but in all cases the individual is being tied to an existence that often prevents them achieving their full potential.

This is not the life that you came on Earth to lead, to work long hours, to give back your money to a bigger power that promises to look after you and give services that it does not deliver on, or to be told that if you cannot or do not have work you are worthless and must only survive on the most meager of incomes. It instills in each and every human on this Earth that there is not enough, that some will have to do without and so the competition begins. And as everyone seeks not to be the one who has to go without, it hardens hearts towards each other so that the idea of helping others or brotherly love as a way of life becomes an idea that cannot be contemplated; fear prevents this – after all there is not enough.

In this way people are controlled; they will not question as they believe they are fighting for their very survival on this planet. By keeping people fearful, hungry, poverty-stricken and fighting among themselves, they can be controlled more easily. They will not seek to question those they perceive to be in authority, they will not refuse to participate in the game and will obediently follow the rules not once stopping to question if there is another way.

But this is all set to change. We can create the life we want to lead. A life which does not involve being at the mercy of others. We can decide by our own positive thoughts and positive intentions what it is and how it is we will live our lives. However, we must also become aware of the beliefs and programs that we hold in our subconscious, and reprogram them to reflect our new lifestyle and beliefs. This may sound very simplistic; in fact it may seem that this could not work, after all the logistics of such a thing would be untenable. How could you have a world where there is more than enough, where there is abundance? You would argue everyone would ask to be rich, famous, to have fast cars, big houses and live a life of ease and idleness. Who would do the more menial tasks, the jobs that people only do now because they need the money? How would society function?

In human terms many people believe that if they have such things as lots of money, big homes or flashy cars then their lives would be perfect; their troubles and worries would be over and they would live happily ever after. The scarcity mentality has emphasized the lack of material wealth as being the monster in the wardrobe, responsible for all misfortunes. In fact it has been identified by many as the sole source of their current unhappiness, so it is natural that for many this pursuit of material wealth becomes the holy grail and the thing that must be attained at all costs. But once attained many will find that this does not bring the satisfaction or gratification that they hoped it would. Instead there may be the fear of keeping it, the fear that even though there appears to be enough at present there may not be enough for all future demands, and as this cycle continues the fear and disease that occurs from separation from the Creator increases and it cannot be replaced by material objects.

In a world of abundance this would not be the case. While in the initial stages people would be consumed with having more, very soon they would grow tired with collecting and start seeking out ways to express their talents or interests. People would choose work that was meaningful to them and gave their life meaning as opposed to working because they had to. This change in attitude would of course be reflected in the way people approached and carried out their work. In this time of change the old corrupt institutions will be washed away, crumble and decay. This is currently happening in much of North Africa and the Middle East; all the major institutions in every country which throughout the years have been accepted as knowing best, as being in complete control, are being revealed for what they are, in many cases incompetent and corrupt. Those who by their positions in such institutions have commandeered our respect and awe are now being shown for what they are: fallible, who are indeed no better or worse than any other human being.

This is what is emerging and each institution will be held up under the spotlight, and those that are not aligned with the ethos and aspirations of the changes sweeping Earth at present will disintegrate under its glare. This too needs to happen because we cannot go forward into a brave new age with these structures in place. In fact such structures would indeed prevent any movement forward in the first instance, and so for a time it may seem that we are left stripped naked, all our certainties gone, all our sureties removed. It would seem we have been given nothing we can cling to for comfort, no one we can turn to for help. This, however, is not strictly true; in fact there is much to be gained from such a place, uncomfortable though it is. This position forces us to look inside to ourselves, to reevaluate, or in some cases for the first time question what it is we want from life, what is important to us, why we are here.

We are beginning to see ourselves not as the 'Masters of the Earth' but as its inhabitants, whose actions have repercussions and who are bound by a series of universal laws that are not manmade but have been in place since time immemorial. This place offers us an opportunity to reconnect with our 'higher self, intuition, superconscious, Universe, Creator' and tap into the guidance that is freely available, and in doing so we can begin to take responsibility for our own lives rather than handing over responsibility to others in perceived positions of power. This position or perspective is very different from the 1980s self-gratification theme prevalent then.

It means we become aware that we are capable of creating the life we want and do so in a way that does not harm others or does not have a detrimental effect on the environment. We realize we can change the world and can begin to create a world in which everyone has enough, where there is no famine, no war, no inhumanity. In short we can create a society where everyone has hope. The next question then is how do we achieve this? The answer is to reclaim control of our mind, removing those beliefs that limit and no longer serve us, to choose to think thoughts that empower us and create positive emotions within us, and to take action in whatever way is meaningful for us. In short we need to become aware of the power of our own thinking...

Part 4

The Power of Thought

Every second of every minute of every day we are producing thoughts. There is never a space where we are not thinking about something that has happened, is happening, we want or as is often more usual, don't want to happen in the future. They can vary from the mundane, 'What do I want for dinner', to the profound, 'What is the meaning of life?' All thoughts are energy and have energy; all have power. These thoughts do not stop once they have been 'created' but travel out from us into our surrounding space and are picked up and interpreted often at an unconscious level by those within the immediate vicinity.

Modern science now believes that the brain is really a transmitter picking up and sending out these energetic thought forms. The reception and interpretation of these thought forms occur on a subconscious level and so we are often unaware of it happening, but it does explain our ability to walk into a room and sense the mood. That 'mood' has been created by the thought forms of the people in that room. A roomful of interviewees with their own anxious and fretful thoughts will have created an apprehensive, uneasy atmosphere while a room of students on the final day of term with thoughts of their long summer break will create an entirely different ambience.

Thoughts are the one thing that we are all capable of generating regardless of our age, sex, level of education, and of which we have an unlimited supply. We can generate thoughts at will and it is a capacity that we have which occurs spontaneously with no apparent effort on our part. No one can order us to stop having thoughts. It is an impossible task for the untrained mind to stop thinking. In fact it is one of the main difficulties faced by those novices learning meditative techniques, trying to stop intruding thoughts and 'turn off the mind'. While our thoughts are our own creation they nevertheless are open to outside influences and are colored by our perceptions of events, people and personal and cultural belief systems. Thoughts are formed in the conscious mind but are directly influenced by the beliefs and attitudes held in the subconscious mind, and are guided and brought into balance by the wisdom and intuitive knowing of the superconscious mind or as it is sometimes referred to the 'higher conscious'.

The mind has been likened to a team of wild horses pulling a chariot. When controlled by the driver (the superconscious mind) the chariot (the conscious) and the horses (subconscious) can navigate all obstacles skillfully, arriving at their destination successfully. When these same horses are allowed to follow their own path then all can land in the ditch! The mind is also open to manipulation by others who may encourage a specific event or person to be perceived in a particular way to ensure certain actions are initiated that benefit the manipulator. The 'mob rule' scenario very ably demonstrates what happens when our collective thoughts are hijacked and are propelled along a route which with thoughtful consideration we may not have chosen as an appropriate reaction to that situation. In this scenario an agitator will feed an already emotionally tense audience a series of thoughts that play on their fears and insecurities, while at the same time encouraging them to take action to prevent such an outcome.

Most people can spend a large part of their lives unaware of the thoughts that they have. They are oblivious to the power within them and that (particularly when coupled with strong emotion) these thoughts in that very instant are helping to create their future. It does not matter whether they are what we deem to be 'good' or positive thoughts or 'bad' negative thoughts; the Universe merely interprets them as expressions or desires of what the person wishes to experience in their life and sets about activating circumstances that will allow their manifestation and actualization.

People have within them the capacity to choose their thoughts and create the feelings and outcomes they want in life. They can learn to control their thoughts rather than allowing their thoughts to control them. In many cases the mind is allowed free rein to lead where it pleases; sometimes it can take the form of idyllic daydreams of how they would like things to be, of the things they would like to achieve or have. This generates pleasant feelings of happiness, satisfaction and well-being. This of itself is not a bad thing as it permits us to step outside the limitations of our own thinking and societal restriction, and to wonder 'What if?' In this space we can imagine how we would feel, or how we would react to being in a situation that at present appears out of reach. It can clarify for us what we want in life, what we would like to achieve and our goals for the future. It allows ideas and inspiration to flow. The imaginative mind is activated and everything is possible as all restrictions are removed. This is the mind working at its best, in a way that uplifts, motivates and empowers, placing us in the role of co-creator in our lives and on this Earth.

We must, however, be mindful that this is not our current reality and that all we are viewing are possibilities that will require change and action on our part if they are to manifest. If we become too attached to this space and allow our thoughts to stray and stay continuously in the world of daydreams then we risk becoming a 'Walter Mitty' type character, deluding ourselves as to how developed our abilities are and what we can currently achieve. It does not take account either of the beliefs or attitudes that we hold in the subconscious that stand in the way of our ever making this scene a reality.

At other times the effect of our thinking can be more immediately destructive as events that happened either recently or in the past are recounted. It is replayed, added to, and soon the mind has created a major incident that bears no resemblance to what actually happened. This causes an emotional reaction of anger, rage, worry, fear and a host of other feelings which increase the stress level within the body. As the body does not recognize the difference between reality and imagination, it then releases the stress hormone cortisol in response to these pictures. This results in us experiencing the physical symptoms of stress including increased heart rate, shallow breathing and muscle tension, and all in response to a picture woven by the mind where one thought has led to another and another with no control imposed. This type of thinking also affects the way in which we react when faced with a similar situation in the future or act when we have an encounter with that particular person again.

The mind by its use of thought manipulates us in many ways, and in both scenarios we are not living in the present moment; we are either living in the future or reliving our version of the past. As Eckhart Tolle in his book *The Power of Now* reminds us, it is only by living in the now do we have the power to affect change in our lives. If we choose to have our attention in the past or the future we can drift through life asleep, unaware of what is truly around us, and oblivious to the opportunities that life is offering us. We can waste much of our time worrying and being irate about things which have never happened, or daydreaming about things which we are not going to manifest into our reality because we believe them to be beyond our capabilities. Mark Twain, when asked if he had any regrets in his life, cited only one, devoting so much time to thinking and worrying about events that never happened or were likely to happen.

All ideas, insights, projects whether big or small begin with a thought. Energy by its very nature is neither good nor bad; it is the meaning that we ascribe to it that makes it empowering or destructive, and it is the strength of the emotion behind that thought that gives it its power. When we consistently think the same thought over and over again it becomes a belief which is stored in our subconscious and is reflected in our response to situations. The Universe, which responds to our every thought, then manifests that belief into our reality. It does not matter whether that thought is life enhancing or destructive, it will be treated the same; it is merely energy. It is the focus on that particular energy form that manifests it into an experience. How many times have we heard people declare: 'This always happens to me!' or 'Bad things always happen to me!' By holding that belief and stating it again and again they ensure that that particular energetic thought form becomes their reality.

Similarly if we think the thought or hold the belief that we are 'very lucky' or 'always find bargains' or 'have a great sense of direction' then the Universe will make that our experience. This gives us a great ability to create our own experiences and lies at the heart of being co-creators with the Divine Universe. It also means that we have to take a certain amount of responsibility for our experience as we can no longer blame people or circumstances when our lives appear not to be working, for we have played a part. Our thoughts have helped attract to us the situations that we are now experiencing.

Thoughts can be a powerful force and should really carry a health warning for if continuously misused they can make us ill both physically and mentally. We are energetic beings and as such cannot escape the effect of energetic thought forms. If we continuously feed ourselves with thoughts that focus on our perceived lack and on everything we think is wrong with us – who we are, what we can achieve, how life is treating us etc. – it is not long before we begin to attach emotions to these thought forms and this is what gives the thought form its power. These thought forms vibrate at a particular frequency and have their own 'vibrational signature' which attract to them people and situations vibrating at a similar frequency. The stronger the emotion and the more passionately we believe in the thought, the more likely we are to manifest a reality that reflects this thought.

These thoughts are welded into a set of beliefs that become part of 'who and what' we consider ourselves to be. They may not initially be of our own making. They can have come from sources outside ourselves: parents, siblings, partners, other family members, in fact anyone who we have encountered in this lifetime, but we have internalized the message and made it our own. A diet of thought forms that focus on our 'wrongness' and perceived weaknesses can lead to loss of self-esteem, depressive thoughts, even to full-blown depression. We become energetically unbalanced, and this can affect both mental and physical well-being.

Many of the mental and physical illnesses that we see today in society have at their core a series of erroneous beliefs that individuals have developed about themselves over the years. Science has proved, and in particular the work of Dr. Bruce Lipton, that there is a molecular connection between thoughts and the physical chemistry of the body to the extent that a negative belief system can actually trigger a genetic marker to initiate the occurrence of disease. Many diseases have in fact begun their life as uncontrolled destructive energetic thought forms that have hardened to become a self-perpetuating reality. There are all too many examples of individuals whose thoughts have caused them to believe that there was no hope, that they were isolated and alone, and had little to offer any one or thing, or indeed that a particular disease ran in their family and there was no escaping it. This has caused many to drift through life feeling a victim of circumstances as opposed to a creator of opportunities.

When thought forms are properly harnessed they can help manifest dreams into realities. The person who is aware of and monitors their thoughts creates a mental attitude in which there are no problems that do not have a solution, there is no adversity which does not hold an opportunity and they truly recognize and believe themselves co-creator with the Divine Creator/Universe.

The same process applies:

- The empowering thought form is created.
- It is powered by the strength of the emotion attached to it.
- It is frequently stated.
- It is internalized as part of the current belief system.
- The Universe responds to it.
- A life-enhancing experience occurs.

Thought forms are one of the building blocks in creating the reality we wish to have. It is our choice whether that thought form is ascribed an empowering or destructive emotion which then determines its effect. The thought 'It's raining' is of itself a neutral statement but depending on the emotion we attach, it becomes either an 'Oh no, it is raining', or 'Whoopee, it is raining!'

As said before time is speeding up; and in direct correlation to that, manifestations are also occurring more quickly, both those that empower and those that are destructive. It is beholden on all individuals on the Earth plane at this time to become more aware of their thoughts and to decide if that thought form is serving them in terms of creating the future they wish to experience or leading them to a place where they are experiencing a range of emotions that cause them to feel disempowered.

It is not that we stop thinking or feeling or indeed cease having disempowering thoughts (it is not possible), but that we are less attached to them. We recognize them for what they are, part of the process of growth. We can feel the loss, betrayal, anger or whatever emotion we need to, after all that is part of what we came on this Earth to experience. It is what makes us human but the difference is we don't define ourselves by it. We do not become our anger, our jealousy, our loss, or whatever prevalent emotion we are feeling. We feel it, and then we release it taking the lesson we have learned from the situation, and using it as a springboard into the next part of our lives; after all what does not kill us will make us stronger.

We have all met or know individuals who have become 'stuck' in an emotion whether it be anger, loss or betrayal who are unable to move on and have as a result of an episode that occurred a long time ago – sometimes 10, 20, 30 years ago – become trapped in the emotion of that incident. It has become 'their anger', 'their loss', 'their betrayal'. They identify totally with this event in a way that justifies to them the decisions they have made in life as all is viewed from this perspective. Their thinking keeps them stuck in a place where their potential is diminished and they are separated from the love and joy of the Source or Divine Universe, and are unable to identify with their own divinity. They remain on an unenviable treadmill where their thought forms attract people and events that essentially confirm the beliefs held in the subconscious mind, and where the superconscious mind or higher conscious is not consulted. They are 'creating', but they are unaware of it; and it is not a reality that they enjoy but one they become used to. They also begin to see themselves as victims in the process of their life as opposed to its creator.

In order to create a world of abundance and hope, we have to go to the source of our individual creation and that is to our thoughts. We must decide what it is that we want to create in our lives. What it is that we sincerely desire, and most important of all we must be sure that we can accept and receive our creation. For instance, there is not much point in wishing to be a millionaire if in our belief system we hold the belief that money is the root of all evil, that it only brings unhappiness and that it is not safe to have a lot of money. We will not be able to manifest in such circumstances, as the subconscious will sabotage all our efforts to succeed in an attempt to 'save' us. Similarly if we desire perfect health but have in our belief system that this is impossible for us because our family has a history of bad health, and it is inevitable and inescapable, then we are not going to be able to create perfect health for ourselves.

The messages that we send to the Universe need to be very clear and specific, for only then can the Universe truly discern our wishes. By focusing on that which we wish to create with empowering thoughts, fuelled by intense, passionate emotion, anything can be achieved. As said, the only limitation we have on our manifestation and actualization is that placed on us by our own belief systems. Some of these beliefs support us through life, but some serve only to keep us trapped in circumstances where we cannot lead the lives we wish. This limiting belief system assures us we seek the impossible, that we are not capable of achieving such things or indeed that our desire will place us in danger. It urges us to give up, convinces us we are better off where we are, and that we are not going to succeed. This message is also received by the Universe, which then makes that our reality.

How then do we become aware of our thoughts, after all we create 70,000 every day; how are we to monitor every thought? The answer is we can't, but we can start to break the pattern by being aware of those thoughts that keep us living in the past, trapped by intense emotions such as anger, jealousy, hatred, sadness or guilt. If we have been someone who has been used to seeing the world through a mist of anger, hurt, or sadness then the ability to monitor our thoughts will not occur overnight, and in fact the subconscious will strongly object to anything that tries to change its viewpoint. The process of dismantling thought patterns and belief systems can take time and needs to be done gently. It does not need to be a traumatic event in which we set out to do battle with the subconscious on a daily or hourly basis, nor does it need to take decades to complete. It begins with simply being aware of the thoughts we are having and a desire to change both them and the patterns of behavior they subsequently provoke.

In asking ourselves 'Do I really believe this?' or 'Is this really the future I wish to create?' we are taking the first steps in identifying our thoughts and breaking the cycle. It gives us space to allow the emotion to dissipate, as our thoughts are what feed that emotion and galvanize us either into action or victimhood. This can be seen in children who in the middle of a huge emotional outburst, perhaps after falling or having something taken away from them, when distracted by something else immediately stop crying to focus on the new stimuli. After a few seconds they recollect what they were doing (i.e. reconnect with the thought pattern) and resume crying albeit with less intensity. The link between the thought 'I have hurt myself' or 'I want that back' and the emotion was temporarily broken and the emotion could not be sustained. As adults we have, with much practice, learned to hold on to that emotion and have stored it for easy access so that we can tap into it at any time a person or event triggers a memory, and the thought pattern or belief contained in that experience.

Within the fields of both Psychology and Psychiatry, it is widely accepted that many of the destructive behaviors engaged in by clients have at their source equally destructive thought forms and belief systems stored in the subconscious. In recent years there are now many techniques that have emerged to work directly on the subconscious, helping change limiting or damaging belief systems and thought forms. Techniques such as Emotional Freedom Technique or the Tapping Process, both of which use a series of Acupressure Points on the various meridians within the body to release beliefs and thought forms held in the subconscious and replace them with other more empowering beliefs. Similarly there are programs that use clearing statements to remove limiting beliefs (Access Consciousness) or audio programs with positive subliminal messaging, which also replaces destructive thought forms held in the subconscious with those that are more beneficial. Hypnotherapy can also change the subconscious programming. Mantras or set phrases can also be used to prevent the mind from initiating a stream of thoughts that will be detrimental to the peacefulness of the individual.

These are but a few of the many tools that can help change the subconscious. All of these techniques can be very useful and many have had great benefit from their use, but we have to take the first step, and that is to become aware of the thoughts we are creating. In that moment, we have to make a decision to either allow the thought to carry on unrestricted and move from the facts of the situation into unfettered projection, fuelled by unbridled emotion; or stop, take a deep breath and ask: 'How are these thoughts making me feel?', 'Are they serving me?', 'Is this the future I wish to experience?' In breathing and concentrating on breathing, you also break the connection between the emotion and the thought, and open a space for the superconscious or higher conscious to be heard by that part of the mind that is directly aligned with the Divine Universe, the Source and from which all wisdom comes. This gesture opens a dialogue among the three parts of the mind and allows a new perspective to enter.

As we do this more and more we will find that the mind begins to respect our requests and that we 'catch' our thoughts before they develop into full-scale dramas. Over time we will change our mental attitude from one of always seeing or preparing for the worst to one of viewing things from a more balanced perspective where we expect the best and see the possibilities in every challenging situation. In Eastern traditions there is the concept of the silent observer, the one who is not the mind but watches and bears witness to the event unfolding. The observer is not sitting in judgment; its role is to be impartial and unattached to what it observes. We all have this capacity to be the observer of what is occurring; in this way we have an opportunity to 'respond to' our experiences as opposed to 'reacting to' situations.

When we react we become the emotion of that particular event, regardless of whether it is empowering or destructive. When we respond we are aware of the emotion but we do not let it lead us into a verbal response or a course of action that we might later regret. This is often epitomized by the Eastern Master who sits undisturbed while all around him are demanding instant action to right a perceived wrong. They are driven by their emotion in that situation which has been triggered, and demand a response that will assuage that emotion. The master, however, considers the facts of the situation and reasons the effects of his actions before deciding on an appropriate response that will be appropriate to that situation. In this way he responds as opposed to reacts, and is in control of the mind not the other way around.

Of course it could be argued that that is why he is a master, and that the rest of us mere mortals would never be able to achieve such serenity in the midst of crisis. Yet that is exactly what happens every day to numerous humans caught in an unexpected drama whether it be an automobile accident or dealing with a medical emergency. They suddenly achieve an inner calmness, become detached from the emotion of the situation and do whatever is necessary to save the day. They may go into shock afterwards but for the moment when they were in that situation they became the observer capable of calm thought and reasoned action.

Becoming aware of and taking control over our thought forms can take time to achieve. The precise length of time will be dependent on how positive or negative your previous thinking has been. It gets easier the longer we practice it. To help achieve this we can begin by spending 10 minutes daily, sitting quietly, being aware of our thoughts as they arise, recognizing them and releasing them without emotion or judgment. In this way we practice being the silent observer and gain insight as to how our mind works. The most important thing to remember is that you are in control. You choose your thoughts, so choose wisely! What follows is a simple exercise for developing awareness of thoughts for you to undertake...

Ask the following questions:

- Is this what I believe?
- Is this thought mine?
- Do I want to create my future based on this thinking?
- How is this line of thinking serving me?

Becoming the Silent Observer:

- Close your eyes.
- Begin by focusing on your breath. Slowly inhale for the count of 5 and exhale for a count of 10.
- Continue to do this 10 times, as you do so allow any thoughts that arise to do so without becoming involved with them.
- Notice them and let them pass, continue breathing.
- As your breathing begins to slow bring your attention to within yourself to that space in your heart, the sacred heart space.
- Hold your attention there for as long as you can again, allow thoughts to arise, notice them but let them pass.

Become the Observer:

- Hold this space for as long as you can before opening your eyes.

With daily practice the length of time you can stay in that quiet space will increase and you will learn to detach from the emotion of thought so that you can observe objectively. The stillness and peacefulness of that space opens the connection with the higher conscious.

Part 5

The Power of Emotions

Emotions are the second building block we use in the manifestation and materialization process. They are the vehicle through which a thought gains its power and meaning. Attaching an emotion to a thought form is the equivalent of igniting the rocket fuel in a spacecraft. The thought form becomes energized and is released into the Universe with purpose in search of recognition and manifestation. The intensity of the emotion coupled with frequent repetition of that particular thought aids its realization.

This is evidenced in the passion and emotional belief that drives many entrepreneurs and sports people to create and succeed even in the face of great adversity and hardship. It is what drives them to take action to practice or work for long hours, to take risks, to make sacrifices, to succeed. They have the thought or idea which is repeated and viewed from every angle, it is visualized, they 'see' themselves achieving their goal. They 'feel' the emotion that achieving their goal will bring and 'be' the person who has achieved that goal. This galvanizes them into taking the action that they know will allow them to achieve the desired outcome.

The same process exists for each of us in our own lives. We may not aspire to win an Olympic medal or be the head of a multimillion-dollar empire, but we have dreams and aspirations that we wish to manifest. We are, whether we realize it or not, activating this process already; the only problem is that we are not aware of it and the emotional passion that we are creating can be harnessing the power of destructive emotions rather than life-enhancing ones. We may have the thought, for example, 'No one ever listens to me.' We create a 'movie' comprising of a series of thoughts, 'seeing' ourselves in situations where we are being actively ignored. We begin to 'feel' the emotion that such a state of affairs would cause and identify with it totally, becoming the person that no one listens to. Our past experience and subconscious belief system are activated and we become passionate about the thought that 'No one ever listens to me.' This is sent out to the Universe, which then sets about creating situations that will mirror this belief.

Emotions are also the key to managing the changes that are occurring at the moment. Our ability to be aware of and choose our emotions in whatever situation we find ourselves ensures that we stay in the eye of the storm as opposed to being swept around in the chaos of the moment, at the mercy of circumstances and the will of others. Our emotions are our most valuable currency in this time of change. Through awareness, choice and purposeful use of emotions, success and happiness are guaranteed for only then can we truly be master of our own destiny. This does not mean we are emotionless (i.e. without emotion). We still feel each emotional state but we have a recognition that we are not that emotion and do not allow ourselves to become defined by that emotion or describe ourselves in terms of that emotion e.g. I am a very happy person. I am a sad or anxious or lonely person.

We have been taught very little about our emotions, their development or the important role they play in our ability to create and sustain a happy life on Earth. In our lifetime we have been given many mixed messages about our own emotions and their expression. They will have been encouraged on occasions, discouraged on others, fully expressed or sometimes totally repressed. As children we have learned that there are good emotions and bad emotions, that some are acceptable, some are unacceptable. We will have been made aware that it is not always 'safe' to express our emotions and that displaying extremes of emotions is frowned on by all.

We have adopted the social behaviors of our family, gender

and culture to fit in, and we express our emotions in socially acceptable ways. If we fail to adhere to these protocols there are consequences. We can be ostracized by those around us, 'earn a reputation' for being different or ascribed a personality to match our emotional behavior e.g. 'Oh he is very hotheaded' or she is a very 'cold' person. However, more and more these emotional constraints are being broken down as ever-increasing numbers of individuals choose not to conform to the social norms. They express their individuality by being open about how they are feeling and sharing that with others. This is a positive step in replacing the suppression of emotion with acceptance of our emotional state.

In one of the more extensive 'happiness' studies done, results indicated that Latino people are generally happier in life than non-Latinos. Researchers concluded that it was not due to just one factor but rather a combination of diet, outdoor living (exposure to more sunshine), strong family values, beliefs and emotional expression (i.e. the freedom to express their feelings). These people feel connected to others and that sense of family and community provides them with an opportunity to express their emotions, release them and move through the situations encountered having been heard and their feelings honored. It is also a cultural norm that expressing emotion is socially acceptable and permitted. This is the opposite to what is so often the situation in other cultures where an incident occurs, emotions are suppressed, go unexpressed and are left to fester in the mind and body. Over time this can lead to mental and emotional imbalance which in the final stages will manifest in the body as dis-ease.

The role of emotions in our life is much misunderstood and we have been given the idea that we should not have or feel what are described as 'negative emotions'. This term is often used to refer to emotions such as anger, sadness, hatred, fear, rage, to name but a few. We have moved from the societal belief that life is a 'vale of tears' to life being the 'Hollywood Dream' as depicted in many films where there is always a happy ending. The implied message is that if we are not feeling happy, joyful, fulfilled all the time then something is wrong either with us or how we are living life.

This does not take account of the fact that we are spiritual beings having a physical experience, and a very important part of that experience is that we get to feel and experience the full range of emotions which in our divine state of unconditional love we would never encounter. They also are an important source of learning when we make choices which take us to a place where we experience a range of emotions that we do not enjoy or are harmful to us. We endeavor in future situations to make choices that will not take us to that place again. In that process we will have learned something about ourselves: the qualities we possess, our strengths and our weaknesses and how we operate in life. Where we operate from a lack of awareness we are destined to make the same choices and return to the same place of 'feeling bad', just by a different route or scenario.

We, as human beings, are privileged to be able to feel and name a wide variety of emotional states. Those such as love, joy, happiness, compassion, bliss, forgiveness and grace add to our sense of Divinity and connectedness to the Creator/Universe or Source. They raise our vibrational level and we are better able to enjoy life and cope with any unexpected situations in a spirit of challenge as opposed to disaster. The positive mindset and sense of well-being that they encourage allows us to find solutions, avoid problems in the first instance and see the learning in everything that occurs. We are operating from a position of power and co-creation.

A similar process occurs with the emotions anger, hatred, jealousy, sadness, guilt, fear. These too affect our well-being; they detract from our sense of divinity and connectedness to the Creator/Source/Universe. When we are wholly involved in these states we feel isolated, alone and often under siege, our vibrational level is lowered and our enjoyment of life suffers. We can easily become overwhelmed by life experiences and get stuck in a rut of destructiveness where we seem to attract nothing but hardship and chaos. It can be very easy to believe that everyone and everything is against us, that we are the victim in the situation, that we have no choices and that we are the emotion that we are experiencing.

However, we need to be aware that the emotion is what we feel, not who we are. Many people can fall into the trap of over identifying with the emotion so they become it. 'I feel angry!' or 'I feel sad' becomes 'I am angry!', 'I am sad' and once that happens we become the emotion that we are experiencing. That one statement gives us permission to act accordingly, so our actions reflect the emotion we are experiencing. This happens regardless of whether that emotion is empowering or destructive, so if we are angry we will act angrily and if we are happy our actions will reflect happiness.

The subconscious mind cannot distinguish between reality in the physical sense and the scenario that we have created in our imagination using our thoughts, and it automatically alerts the body which alters the physiology to reflect that particular emotion. If angry our heart rate increases, our breathing becomes quicker and shallower, hormones are released, the temperature in our body rises causing the smallest blood vessels (capillaries) in our bodies to dilate and move closer to the surface of the skin in order to cool the body down. We get red in the face and can begin to perspire becoming all 'hot and bothered'. Our muscles tense and if the anger is particularly strong they vibrate with tension hence we 'shake with anger'.

When we feel joyful our bodies also change physiologically. Our pulse rate slows, we breathe more deeply allowing more oxygen into the body to carry more nutrients around the body and more toxins from the body, endorphins are released from our hormonal system into our brain which create a feeling of well-being, and our muscles relax. Every single cell in our body is reacting to the emotion that we have allowed ourselves to feel. These transformations happen not once a day, but many thousands of times a day. On a daily basis we swing between empowering and destructive emotional states, and each of these emotional states carries with it a physiological and hormonal response. We often only become aware of it when we have extremes of emotions, the anxiety attack, the big argument, the major fright. We are unaware of the majority of these changes in our physiology because the body does such a magnificent job in maintaining its balance.

This concept of the body being directly affected by emotion is not new, although we now have the scientific evidence that it is so. In Traditional Chinese Medicine which is estimated to be 2000 years old the masters recognized the negative impact that excessive and prolonged exposure to what in some cases might be termed negative emotions have on the internal organs of the body. Each internal organ is said to be directly affected by a specific emotion: the Lung is associated with grief, the Heart with love, the Kidney with fear, the Liver with anger, the Spleen with worry. If an individual experiences that particular emotion for too long or too intensely, then the balance of the Qi and subsequently the physical body becomes upset and other organs affected. It is then that certain acupuncture points or herbal preparations can used to balance the Qi or life force and hence the body. In fact it is regarded by some doctors of Traditional Chinese Medicine that the source of all disease in the body originates from disturbances in the 'Shen' or mind, which lead to emotional disturbances affecting the physical organs of the body and hence the flow of Qi.

After an emotional outburst of whatever nature we can quite quickly 'calm down', 'chill out', 'let it go' – in other words we return to an emotional and physiological equilibrium and carry on; but this is not the case for all individuals and some can get stuck in a particular mode of thinking where thought forms become more fixed and the emotions that they engender become much stronger, lasting for prolonged periods of time. This can be beneficial if we remain in a positive or empowering emotional state for then we go from strength to strength creating and drawing to us our wishes and desires; this can be a period of great achievement and creation. Many artists have these creative periods when they can work for hours in a heightened state of bliss and euphoria unaware of the time passing and totally focused on the work in hand. They have tapped into a vibrational frequency that allows their creativity to flow and the joy that such an episode causes is treasured when it occurs.

However, for other people, they become trapped in a cycle of destructive thought patterns and emotions which if severe and prolonged can cause an imbalance in both their mental and emotional state and bodies. In the more acute cases it can become extremely difficult for their physical body to achieve that almost instantaneous homeostatic balance and a prolonged chemical imbalance occurs, necessitating in some cases medical intervention to restore the balance to allow the individual to function fully in life again. The hormones being released into the bloodstream are released for a longer than necessary period of time and lock the body into a stressed, agitated state responding to all incidents as if they were highly pressurized and stressful occurrences. The mind which seeks to explain the physical symptoms of the body creates thought patterns based on unseen potential threats. This transfers into the individual's behavior, and activities that under normal conditions would be regarded as mundane become high stress. A trip to the supermarket to pick up some milk suddenly becomes a mammoth journey fraught with anxiety, trepidation and in more severe cases all out panic.

Similarly if endorphins are released for too long a feeling of ecstatic euphoria can emerge that leaves the individual unable to adequately respond to situations, unaware of danger, oblivious to their surroundings and personal limitations. In such a florid state some undertake commitments and become involved in actions that are detrimental to both themselves and others. Both these scenarios represent extremes but are examples of the symbiotic relationship between the emotional aspect of our being and the physical body (particularly the endocrine system which governs the production and secretion of hormones) and how imbalances in one can adversely affect the other.

As we continue through this period of change and transition, levels of personal as well as societal stress are increasing, more people are seeking help to cope with what from a medical perspective are identified as 'mental illnesses'. These can include such conditions as depression, bipolar disorder, psychosis, eating disorders, self-harming, paranoia etc., all of which carry a defined set of symptoms that refer to the individuals' mental state.

Depression is one of the better known conditions and one which is becoming more openly talked about as many individuals seek help with feelings that leave them debilitated, unable to function in life, devoid of hope, happiness and love. It is a medical term which in psychiatry is defined as a morbid sadness, dejection or melancholy. The individual is cut off from those feelings that give life meaning and fulfillment and are, as some describe, trapped in a black hole of despair from which they cannot escape or see an ending to. Winston Churchill famously referred to his depression as the 'black dog' that followed him around.

While the word 'depression' may describe the symptoms that people feel, it does not explain the cause or origins of the condition. There are many triggers ranging from traumatic and abusive life experiences that have robbed the individual of their self-esteem, self-worth and self-love, to disappointments in life circumstances where expectations have not been met and have left the person feeling inadequate, unloved, a failure. At the core of the problem is a set of beliefs that are no longer serving the individual, magnified by emotions that create a distortion in the individual's perception of themselves and who they really are. They are unaware or unable to connect with the concept that they are a divine being of unlimited potential with the power to use their thoughts, words, emotions and actions to create the life that they wish to have. They define themselves by the emotions that they feel in that particular instant or sometimes don't feel depending on the severity of the depression, and as a result find themselves the victim in the emotional state that they are experiencing.

One of the more insidious effects of depression is the belief that there is no escape or hope. Historically the medical response to depression has been to try and rectify the chemical imbalance with either antidepressants to 'lift' the mood or suppressants to numb the feelings, or a combination of both. This is done in the belief that humans are biochemical organisms and that by restoring the chemical balance all will be well; 'talk therapies' such as counseling or psychoanalysis may also be offered to try and discover why they feel the way they feel. While these approaches may work for some people, for others it has led them to lifelong dependence on medication or years of analysis, focusing on 'their problems'. The individuals begin to think of themselves in terms of a label or condition – 'I am bipolar' – and this can leave little room for empowering thoughts that will help them know themselves as the divine being and that they are capable of achieving anything they desire. Modern medicine is beginning to accept that one of the most potent prognostic factors in a patient's recovery is whether they believe they will get well or not. This belief consists of empowering thoughts fuelled by a positive emotional state which charges the body with the task to create health and balance.

The challenge is to become aware of how our emotional

system works and use it to our advantage to enhance a belief system made up of thoughts that are life enhancing coupled with positive emotional states that energize and fuel these beliefs. It is a fact of life that we will all encounter emotional states from time to time that will knock us out of balance and cause us to question who we are or rather who we think we are. These episodes are often triggered by challenging circumstances in which those beliefs that we have accepted from others do not work in the situations we find ourselves in. This engenders feelings of worthlessness, of being incapable, unlovable, alone in our difficulties; however, such episodes where everything feels so dreadful may actually be a period of transformation where by going through what are often deemed negative emotions we come through this period stronger and onto a new level of understanding and knowing.

These 'negative emotions' are part of our emotional makeup and indeed part of what we, as spiritual beings, came on Earth to experience, so we cannot escape or avoid them nor should we; they are a crucial and vital aspect of our experience on Earth. In the past there has been a 'belief' that spiritual development was dependent on having no 'negative emotions' and that to experience such emotions was indeed a failure, was not being 'spiritual'. Those who were seeking enlightenment often sought to suppress any strong emotions. Emotions such as anger and rage were repressed and pushed down in the belief that a state of inner peace was being achieved and those emotions had been controlled, annulled, transformed; however, this was not always the case and they often reappeared with a vengeance when least expected, causing greater damage. It was the role of the Guru to help the disciple discern when the emotion had been truly transmuted or when it had been merely repressed. Happily there is now a greater understanding of the value of experiencing all emotions and the power that they bring when fully experienced and transformed. The greatest damage we can do to ourselves and our energetic body is to suppress our emotions; in doing so we create toxic energy that causes imbalances not only in the emotional and mental aspects of our being, but eventually settles in the physical body causing 'dis-ease'.

The question is – what do we do once we find ourselves experiencing emotions that we consider to be 'negative'? How do we use these emotions to our advantage? The first step is to acknowledge the emotion that we are feeling. If we can name the emotion then we immediately become more in charge of it rather than the other way around; for instance by stating 'I am perceiving sadness or happiness or anger or anxiety' that statement can reduce the potency of that emotion and allows us distance from it. We have acknowledged its presence and part of us has become the silent observer watching. We allow ourselves to feel the emotion without becoming it, recognizing we are not the emotion we are feeling, that this is a transient phase which will pass and finally using that emotion to create something better. If we can use what we term 'negative' emotional states in a creative way by harnessing the power and intensity behind them to motivate us into purposeful action, then we are in control of them rather than the other way around.

If for example we watch something on TV, perhaps an image of a famine-torn area, and become angry at how that famine is affecting the children of that particular area. We will feel angry; now we have a choice – we can bang doors, rant about the unfairness of life, the corruption and incompetency that allowed this to happen in the first place or turn that anger into action, organize a fund-raising activity for the area, set about galvanizing others to get involved in helping that area; in other words use that anger as a means of empowerment to take positive action rather than allowing the emotion to further the belief that life is unfair but there is nothing you can do about it. In short we can use every emotional state to create something positive. In this way we can deal with the circumstances that we encounter in life in a more effective way. We will be less likely to attract destructive experiences as our vibrational level will cause us to operate in a different space from those situations; or where we do find ourselves in a negative emotional state we will more quickly become aware of what we are feeling and move ourselves to a more life-enhancing state.

'Emotional Intelligence' is a term which has gained in popularity in the last few decades and came to prominence with the creation and publication of the book *Emotional Intelligence* by Daniel Goleman in 1995. The essential premise of Emotional Intelligence (EQ) is that success requires the effective awareness, control and management of one's emotions, and those of other people. Goleman identified five domains which were key to emotional intelligence:

- Knowing your emotions.
- Managing your own emotions.
- Motivating yourself.
- Recognizing and understanding other people's emotions.
- Managing relationships, i.e. managing the emotions of others.

He argued that by developing EQ in all the above domains not only would we become more productive and successful at what we do but we would help others to become more productive and successful. Research also been shown that the process and outcomes of Emotional Intelligence development also contain many elements known to reduce stress for individuals and organizations, by decreasing conflict, improving relationships and understanding, and increasing stability, continuity and harmony. It is now an integral part of many large corporations' interviewing process as it is recognized that academic achievement on its own is not a sufficient criteria for necessarily getting the best person to achieve the task.

It is surprising then that given the body of evidence there is as to the importance of emotional intelligence and its effect on the well-being of both the individual and society that mainstream education has, as yet, devised no formal teaching for the development of this crucial ability. In the temples and ashrams of the Eastern world this is indeed what the initiates underwent, training that allowed them to develop an awareness of and control of their emotions. They became masters of their emotions and often their teachers manipulated situations so that the student could test their mastery of the emotions by ordering them to perform tasks that in today's modern world would be considered mindless, exploitative, and even cruel.

There is a story of the ancient Buddhist Master Marpa who was approached by a would-be initiate who wanted to be his student to appease for previous wrongdoing. Before agreeing Marpa ordered him to build a house of stone which the initiate duly did; when it was completed he enquired what he would do now. Master Marpa's answer was to that he take it down stone by stone; that done the enquiry was made as to what next, the answer was to build it again and so the pattern was repeated until Master Marpa was satisfied that he had a student who was capable of learning as during that process the student had demonstrated patience, diligence, acceptance and non-attachment to outcome. He had learned to control his thoughts and emotions and was now ready to receive sacred teachings.

In this modern world we may well be assured that we are surrounded by chaos but we need not necessarily be in it or affected by it. Central to this is our awareness of and ability to control our emotions. The moment we cease to be in control of our emotions, they will control us and we must be prepared to accept the consequences of such an alliance. The newspapers and television reports are full of stories where, in an instant, individuals allowed their emotional state to influence their actions and in that moment their lives were changed forever.

Their lawyer will argue that their client acted out of character, or they were temporarily insane. The person cannot explain their action; they don't know what happened or why they acted in such a manner. All they are aware of is that now they have to live with the consequences of their action and for some that can be lifelong. Sometimes their actions will have been fuelled by drugs or alcohol, which temporarily numb the link between the individual and that divine aspect of him/herself (the Higher Self). In this state they can feel such extremes of destructive emotions that they do not care what they do to themselves or others. At that point the future does not matter; they have no sense of hope, connectedness or self-love. They have allowed themselves to become their emotional state and have acted out that state. They have no choice now but to accept the path that their actions have led them to.

Emotions are the most powerful tools that we as humans have at our disposal to navigate our way through the experiences we create and encounter in our journey through life. They are the means by which we can with thought forms become co-creators. They have an inherent power which we must be aware of and respect, for their use will ultimately decide how we live our life on this planet. The majority of people travel through life with their emotional barometer turned off.

The experiences of life have left many feeling emotionally deadened; many of these traumas can have occurred very early in our life but their emotional legacy is with us today and affects how we deal with everyday situations. This 'emotional baggage' also stops us from seizing our power as co-creators, for we have been led to believe that we have not the ability to create the life we want. Such is the power of emotional beliefs that some do not dare to even contemplate what they want in life. They accept what happens to them without the understanding that they are actually creating this reality and that they have the power to make changes in both their thinking and how they react to and in situations.

If we can develop an awareness of what we are feeling in the various situations in which we find ourselves by asking the question 'How is this making me feel?' or 'What am I feeling?' then we are giving ourselves an opportunity to review and possibly change the emotion we are ascribing to that event. We switch from being a victim of our emotions to being master of them. This again will involve mindfulness, awareness and purpose, but will become more automatic with time and practice. There are also a myriad of programs that can be used to both identify and remove emotionally-based patterns of behavior that are no longer serving us including Emotional Freedom Technique, Tapas Acupressure Techniques, Access Consciousness, The Sedona Method, to name but a few. It is never too late to begin developing your emotional mastery and there are no limits to the levels you can develop. It is yet another key in helping to create the life you desire. I pose the following questions to help gain insight into Emotional Patterns...

- What am I feeling?
- Do I enjoy feeling like this?
- What other emotion could I choose in this situation?
- What other possibilities are available to me right here, right now?
- What would the Divine Creator do/feel in this situation?
- What is stopping me from choosing a more empowering emotion?

Part 6

The Power of Intention & the Spoken Word

The word 'intention', when broken down, means 'intent on', and it brings focus to our actions, allowing us to be creators and manifest in our lives that which we wish to have. It is very much linked to our subconscious, and since intention has no preference of its own, it will create and manifest that which we put our intention and focus on. While this may seem like a wonderful thing (which it is) it also comes with a caution, for whether that focus is on empowering or destructive thoughts and emotions it will manifest that without any judgment. This is why it is so important to be aware of our emotional reactions to experiences and circumstances, for what we are 'intent on' or focus on will grow, be it something we wish to create or something which we fear and want to avoid.

As in gardening if we lavish loving care and attention on plants they will grow; if we add fertilizer to that process they will grow much quicker. In our applying of the fertilizer we may pour some inadvertently on nearby weeds; they too will flourish. It does not matter whether we pour fertilizer on flowers or weeds; we increase their growth. The fertilizer does not discriminate; it just does its job. Intention is the fertilizer for thoughts regardless of whether those thoughts are empowering or destructive. It intensifies the process, allowing manifestation and material-ization to occur more quickly as it is often the precursor to taking action. What attention and focus will create after an extended period of time, intention will create and manifest in half that time; this makes it a very potent force to be handled wisely.

When we make something our intention, or state it is our intention to do something, have something, or create something, then we set in place a series of cosmic events that will manifest in our lives. We have entered into a contract with the Universe which states that we wish to create a certain event or experience in our life. How it occurs may not be in exactly the way that was envisaged but it will occur in a way that will epitomize the ethos of what was intended. We are making a commitment, setting a goal, giving any actions that we may take focus and power. It is not so much a case of 'be careful what you wish for' as 'be careful what you make your intention'.

Intention is a much stronger force than wishes, wants or desires. When we express our desire or wish to have or do something there is implicit in that the possibility that we may not receive what we want. We may be deflected from our course of action, or procrastinate around taking action to achieve what we have expressed. There is an unspoken possibility or belief that wishes do not always come true. However, when we verbally express an intention there is much more power behind that decision; we are making a pledge both to ourselves and the Universe and are as a result much more likely to initiate the action necessary to make that intention a reality, as we have the support of the Universe to help make it happen.

Intention is really at the heart of goal setting; when we decide on our goals or what it is we hope to achieve we are really making a series of intentions encapsulated in a time frame. In making an intention there are four parts to it: the first is the thought followed closely by the words that we use to express that intention and then the emotion and the passion that we create to drive that intention into the final stage action. Each one of these parts is vitally important if that intention is to become a reality. As in any plan, failure to take adequate action will affect the results obtained. The old adage that 'the road to hell is paved with good intentions' very much reflects what happens when the last two stages are omitted. However, the first two stages are equally important, not only the original thought but the words used to express that thought.

As humankind has evolved over the centuries, it has become much more fluent in the use of language, moving from primal grunts to an ability to use language to describe objects or events, convey emotions, predict and discuss abstract thoughts and ideas. Along the way it has lost the knowledge that words have power, and that often it is not only in the actual words themselves but also in the intention behind the words. This was very much known by the ancient peoples, the Egyptians, the Mayans, the Aztecs whose priests and priestesses used particular invocations or words to invoke the power of their Gods. They had a belief that each one of these words had power and that only by saying these words in a certain way using a certain order could that power be released. This is the same belief found in the Vedic texts of ancient India, where specific syllables hold certain powers and when arranged into a mantra that the power can be released by the individual uttering them. The use of spells and charms by those practicing 'magic' or Wicca is well documented. These practices recognize and are reliant on the power of words for their successful execution.

In everyday situations we can all distinguish between the person who wishes us well and actually means it from the heart, and the person for whom these are empty words or those who really wish us ill. They all use the same words but all have different meanings as the intention behind the utterance varies. The Native Americans had their own phrase to describe this behavior where the speaker was accused of speaking with a 'forked tongue', hiding their true intention behind words meant to deceive. Words uttered from the heart with a clear intention have a greater power regardless of who utters them, than those used with no intention. The idea of 'small talk' very much demonstrates this phenomenon where a conversation is engaged in but it is empty, devoid of emotion, passion or intention. It is used to acknowledge the presence of another individual but the words hold no power within them, and so the connection between the individuals is minimal.

Words can create and unleash strong emotions that are empowering or destructive. We all know the effect words of love, encouragement, appreciation or gratitude have on us, and on how they make us feel firstly about ourselves and then about the person saying them. The power of such words is immediately felt, our heart opens and we feel a deep and loving connection with the person saying them; we are inspired to be the best we can be, to realize our full potential. We feel appreciated and our efforts recognized. For some who have not been used to hearing such words, this experience can be disconcerting, even emotional as feelings of worthlessness and hurt are released. We can be unsure of how to react, how to respond or what to do with this information initially, but such words can be the beginning of a healing process. Similarly words of contrition or forgiveness can be the first steps in repairing broken or strained relationships.

Words of anger, rage, or jealousy also have great power, but are often used in a more destructive, negative way that does great harm to both the person using them and those they are directed at. And in our modern age we have become careless with our words and more importantly the intention behind them. We pay little regard to what we say, how we say it or the effect that our words have on others. It is commonplace to hear people describe how they unleashed their frustration and anger on some hapless worker who had happened to represent an institution or company that they were angry at.

Such incidents are recounted with pride, with little awareness that that employee does not make policy and as a human being will have been affected by the barrage of abuse that has been hurled at them. Words can be used in a violent manner and can do as much damage to the psyche and well-being of that individual as a physical assault. In fact many instances of violence are preceded by episodes of verbal insults and abuse. It is only in recent times that the phenomenon of mental and emotional abuse is being recognized as a criminal act and the weapon of choice are words which are intended to wound and hurt.

In times past there was a sense of honor associated with words. A man's word was 'his bond' in that if he said something he meant it, if he gave an undertaking to do something then he would do it. The intention behind the word was true; it was a bond of trust. In these times this sense of honor and trust has been diluted. There are many for whom their word has no value; they say one thing while all along intending to do something quite different to what they have said. These 'empty promises' are quite common. Their word has neither honor nor trustworthiness, and this is reflected in how they live their lives and the people and situations they draw into their lives.

What these individuals are doing is essentially 'telling lies'; they are willfully using an untrue statement to deceive another. While we may strive to tell the truth, the whole truth and nothing but the truth, this we know is not always the case. There are times when to tell the 'whole truth' may be detrimental to an individual or a situation. It would not be of any benefit on the morning of a wedding in response to the bride's question 'How do I look?' to tell her you do not like her dress. Similarly as many partners will testify, the question 'Do I look fat in this?' has to be handled with diplomacy and tact if relations are to be maintained.

In such instances, are we telling the truth or giving an opinion? We essentially are giving our opinion on our perception of the situation and our own preferences. These 'little white lies' are generally seen as being harmless and acceptable as they hurt no one and allow others to feel good about themselves. However, as we go further up the scale of telling lies it has a cumulative effect and people do begin to get hurt. The partner who has an affair and lies to conceal it, or the employee who uses words with the intention of hiding the fact that they are embezzling from their company. Eventually we have lying on a national and international level.

A recent example of this was the global financial crisis which when traced back to its origins involved financial traders selling to others financial packages that included subprime mortgages that they knew were problematic. This 'off-loading' was deemed acceptable practice by those involved – it was after all 'business' – but when one looks at the issues involved, essentially one party entered into a contract making 'false promises' with the intention of deceiving the other to make a profit. The consequence of such dubious business practices was that many Western economies were thrown into chaos, and the populations of the various countries have had to pay for the financial traders' deceitful behavior.

Politicians are another group of professional individuals who tend to bear the wrath of the nation not only because of the actions that they take in the name of democracy, but because they are seen as untrustworthy. This stems from the belief that they are not men/women of their word; that they make promises to get elected, but once in power they recant on their election promises, and so are not to be trusted. It would seem that on some level there is a general recognition that 'our word' needs to be honored.

Another misuse of words within our present society is the commonplace practice of 'cursing others', using profanities and generally wishing ill on people with little regard to the impact that this has on their own energy fields. In medieval times to curse or be the subject of a curse was a serious matter. There was the general recognition that such an event had repercussions which could interfere with the 'luck' enjoyed by the family. Today this is regarded as mere superstition and the product of ignorance and folklore; however, there may be a grain of truth in this once widely-held belief. We sometimes utter curses as a joke – 'I hope you crash' – believing that it is a harmless piece of fun, or we utter it in the heat of an argument – 'I wish I was dead' –

and think it is of no consequence. Unfortunately, the subconscious does not recognize humor, nor the fact that we really didn't mean it.

It doesn't understand that we are merely 'having a laugh' or 'getting even'; it processes the words as they are said and stores the information as a desire for a crash or to die. It is added into the mix that helps form our belief system and create our own energetic vibrational signature. As we go through this time of change those profanities and destructive intentions add to the chaos around us. They build up negative and destructive energy that can wreak havoc in our daily lives, attracting to us negative situations that mirror the negative intentions; so in a strange way they may affect our 'luck'.

Inherent in the cursing of another is a lack of generosity of spirit; we are hoping and intending that harm befall the individual so that he or she may not reach their potential or have abundance, peace, or joy in their lives. We want things to be difficult for them, but in doing this to others we also attract the same difficulties into our own lives. This concept of generosity of spirit is quite alien in our modern-day world where competition has been the name of the game. We have all been led to believe, from a very young age, that it is a 'dog eat dog' world out there, everyone is your competitor and in order to get ahead you have to be strong, eliminate the competition or opposition before they eliminate you. This ethos has also been mirrored in modern business practices, which have sought to destroy the competition by whatever means necessary.

In this environment it is easy to see how words can be used to damage that competition: the well-placed rumor, the cleverly worded ad campaign that seeks both to bamboozle the public while at the same time undermining the competition. Underlying this lack of generosity is the notion that there is not enough to go around, and that someone or something will have to do without. This viewpoint has strengthened the idea of separation and does little to promote the idea of oneness among humanity.

It has long been acknowledged that cooperation achieves so much more than competition and promotes a healthier and happier population; unfortunately when 'cooperation' has been entered into by many large conglomerates or countries it has resulted in 'cartels' that have sought by their sheer size to control a resource or influence the direction of policy for their own particular gains. This is not the cooperation that underlies generosity of spirit; it rather is the manipulation of circumstances and people for particular or personal gains, as opposed to a cooperation that will benefit all including the planet. When we embrace true generosity of spirit it is a heartfelt delight in the good fortune or progress of others; it is a willingness to share ideas, resources or time with others so that through collaboration a greater potential can be realized.

Throughout history there have been individuals who by the power of their words and intention have been able to influence millions of people into thinking something different, to imagining a different reality, to let go of their limiting beliefs and take action to create a better life for not just themselves but for the benefit of all of humankind. These individuals are often regarded as being the great orators of their time. Dr. Martin Luther King (Jr.), who by the power of his word urged others to share his 'dream' and in that moment he 'moved' a nation to visualize a different society in which all were regarded as equal. That visualization galvanized a complete generation of Black Americans and their more liberal white counterparts into action to create that vision.

Similarly Winston Churchill at a time of great fear and despair during the Second World War inspired a nation to move from that fear of invasion and imminent death to a place of empowerment with his 'we will fight them on the beaches' speech. A more recent example was the acceptance speech of Barak Obama on becoming the first black president of America.

He through his words inspired a nation, which had been become disillusioned by the experiences of recession, being involved in two foreign conflicts, people losing both their jobs and homes, that there was hope and that together they could create a new and better future under the slogan of 'Yes we can'.

When we use our 'word energy' in a way that benefits those around us we nourish and honor the divinity that is within each and every one of us regardless of appearance. We step out of our limitations and begin to reclaim the power of our spoken word to manifest that which we desire to materialize. Florence Scovel Shinn in her book *The Power of the Spoken Word* cites the power of the spoken word as "one of the most important tools" in successfully attaining what you wish to acquire in this life. She describes many instances when by the sheer power of and belief in the 'spoken word' circumstances were changed, desired outcomes achieved and disasters averted. Words were fashioned into affirmations, which essentially are a series of words arranged into statements that reflect that which we wish to have as our reality. They are then repeated on a frequent basis with the intention of having those affirmations manifest into reality. They can be on any topic whether to increase material wealth or health, to bring about a desired change in circumstance or an improvement in a relationship.

All that is important is that you truly desire the change and believe in the power of the spoken word or affirmation, repeat it often and have faith it will come about either exactly as you have determined or in a way that is even better. You accept the outcome knowing you are always being taken care of, and your highest good is the final outcome. In adopting this stance you are more likely to allow these words to influence your thoughts, emotions and direct the actions you take to achieve your target. It once again is not a matter of uttering an affirmation and then sitting waiting for it to arrive.

One further consideration with regard to affirmations that can interfere with their manifestation is the personal beliefs held either on a conscious or subconscious level. We may on a conscious level believe in a particular affirmation; however, on a subconscious level hold a belief that is diametrically opposed to that affirmation. If for instance we make the affirmation or intention that 'I want a loving relationship' but we hold in our subconscious the beliefs that 'I am unlovable' or 'I am not capable of having a relationship they always end in disaster', then it will be more difficult to create the loving relationship that you truly desire.

The beliefs that you hold must be dealt with first. They may not be held at a conscious level, they may not even be yours but you have unconsciously integrated them into your own belief system. When you create an affirmation, wait for a second and listen for the thoughts that come into the mind. Do not judge them, rather write these thoughts down; this will give you access to the belief system that is running your life and then remove them either one by one or as a complete package. This can be done by speaking directly to your subconscious, reading the old belief aloud and stating that you are changing that belief by saying, 'I now choose to believe...', replacing it with your new belief or using a clearing statement to remove that belief. There are a myriad of methods and systems available aimed at creating change within the subconscious belief system e.g. Access Consciousness.

We have now reached a stage in our evolution where these changes can occur instantaneously and do not have to take years to complete. By identifying the beliefs you hold and clearing those that no longer serve, you are more likely to avoid the self-sabotaging behaviors which prevent the affirmations from being effective, so it is important to take time to do this work.

When we acknowledge the divinity in another person, using words that hold the intention of speaking with love from the heart, a wonderful thing happens. We give the other person an opportunity to respond from a new perspective. So often our conversations are based on what we think is going to happen, how we expect someone to act or react. We do not see our conversations as being fresh and new; we adopt a role and expect the other person to react to that role. When we speak from the heart we rewrite the script, in fact we throw it out, and for those with expectations around us, while they may continue in their old patterns for a time, they will slowly begin to change their way of communicating as their predictions are not met. Others will seize the opportunity to step out of their designated role and speak in a way that more truly reflects what they feel rather than the role they have been playing.

When we sit down for a 'heart to heart' we identify that this type of communication is different from any of the other conversations we may have. It involves being open, honest and direct about how we feel about an issue, what we need, and how we are going to move forward. There is an unspoken agreement that both parties will be honest and participate fully, that there will be no pretending or creating wrong impressions. This way of talking allows us to raise our vibrational frequency and communicate in a way that is meaningful, uplifting and from the heart.

This method of conversation tends to be the exception rather than the rule, and is regarded as being the remit of special occasions or only to be used in crisis situations. We may limit this form of communication to a few individuals that we feel we trust and will respect our confidence. In such encounters we are more likely to tell it how it is and not try to present it in a different light to make ourselves look better or preserve that image that we are projecting to the world. We allow our vulnerability to emerge, and stop deluding ourselves and others. This often is a relief that all is out in the open and everyone can stop pretending. Solutions are more easily found, decisions more easily taken and action more directly taken when we operate from the heart.

That does not mean that such a process does not involve

emotional discomfort, it can and it does; but if all involved are speaking from the heart then no one is in any doubt about how the other feels. There is less second-guessing, misunderstanding, recrimination, or guilt, all of which are harmful and prevent the onset of healing. The breakup of a relationship, business partnership or friendship is never easy, but in talking from the heart we reduce the amount of emotional damage that can occur in such circumstances.

The way in which we use words has a profound effect on the experiences we draw to ourselves and helps define the relationships we have with all aspects of life including finances, health, career and personal relationships. When we begin the sentence 'I am ...' we are giving a direct instruction to the Universe of what it is we are or intend to be, so it is vitally important that this phrase is followed by a positive adjective 'I am healthy', 'I am happy' etc. If we begin our day with the intention of using words that empower us and others we are less likely to be drawn into gossip or speaking destructively about others or the situations in which we find ourselves. In this way we are more likely to choose more empowering thoughts and emotions that allow us to focus on the opportunities which life presents as opposed to the difficulties.

We may use words to mislead others sometimes even ourselves, but we will not deceive the Universe as to the intentions behind those words. If we can speak from the heart in all our encounters however difficult this may be initially, we will find ourselves communicating in a more meaningful and inclusive way with others. We will also reduce the amount of harmful 'self-talk' we engage in. This change in communication also affects how others communicate with us, for what we give out we get back. This allows us to create a more harmonious environment for ourselves and others, one in which we give and receive love and respect, and manifest into reality the life that we wish to create, for by our words so are we known.

The following are questions that we can consider when in conversation with others...

- Is this self-talk empowering me? If not, what words can I choose to change it?
- Is this conversation that I am having making me feel good about myself and or the situation? If not, what words can I choose to change it?
- What words can I choose that would change this conversation into one that is more uplifting for everyone involved?
- Am I willing to be vulnerable in conversation with this person, and speak from the heart?
- Do I really want to be part of this destructive conversation?

Part 7

The Power of Faith

At our disposal in managing change and creating the life we wish is 'faith' and its physical expression, 'prayer'. Faith can be defined as a belief or set of beliefs made up of thoughts and ideas that have been frequently repeated and bound together with the strong emotion of certainty, but it is actually more than this. It is a certainty born of an inner knowing that a course of action or indeed an individual is worth believing in. It allows humans to have faith in their own ability to achieve, as in 'self-belief', or in a greater force outside of themselves that is capable of helping to achieve their aims and goals.

In self-belief we have faith in ourselves, we encourage and motivate ourselves into action with positive self-talk and visualizations in which we either imagine ourselves achieving our goal in the future or we reflect on our successful past achievements. This allows us to take the risk, make the commitment, or commence the actions to achieve our goals and create the desired outcome. If we have faith in our own abilities and believe that we have the power to achieve whatever we have set for ourselves, then we are recognizing our own divinity and the talents and abilities that we all have come to this Earth with.

When we lose faith in ourselves we are discounting those talents and abilities, and are making judgments about ourselves. It is those judgments that prevent us from reaching and experiencing our potential. The judgments that we hold color the view that we have of ourselves, the world we live in and our ability to function in that world. They serve to limit us and ensure that we never step out of the reality that has been created for us, and never contemplate what else we could achieve or that there are other possibilities in which we could engage.

So where do these judgments come from? Were we born with them? Did we come to realize them all by ourselves or were they given to us over a period of time by those around us and by society in particular? The latter is of course true – we are born with incredible self-belief and faith in ourselves. As a child we think there is nothing that we cannot be, achieve or choose; as we go through life there is a never ending line of individuals and institutions to tell us what is possible or not possible, what we can or can't do. The reasons given can vary, that we have not the skills, ability or lack a certain quality needed, that the family that we are born into would not approve of our choice, or that because of our gender, age, or social background a particular choice is not available. Little by little as we accept these viewpoints as truths our choices are eroded, we begin to doubt our abilities and, even more damaging, begin to believe the judgments that are placed upon us.

We live our lives according to these judgments and it is seems the Universe is only too happy to provide us with experiences that corroborate these beliefs. It is difficult in the face of what we consider to be irrevocable evidence to have faith in our own abilities as a divine being, and to believe that we can create a life of our choosing. If we have faith in a power outside ourselves we trust that although we have no physical evidence of its existence it is there and that it has our best interests at heart. We are using an inner knowing that there is something greater than ourselves.

The means used to contact this greater power known by whatever name (God, Allah, Buddha, Divine Creative Force, the Creative Force, the Universe or Source) is prayer which is one of the oldest means of communicating with this Divine Creative Force. In its original form it was the direct connection from the individual to that aspect of self, the 'higher self', which was directly aligned with this Divine Creative Force. It was the means by which the individual remained at one with the Divine Creative Force through conversing from the heart.

Over time the term 'prayer' has come to refer to a prescribed form of communication which lies at the core of all religious practice and usually consists of a set series of words to be used in a particular way to speak directly with the Divine Creative Force/God. It has been implied that only by invoking these words in the manner taught can one 'talk to' the Divine Creative Force. This can mean that for many, prayer becomes an act of repetition of words repeated so often that they cease to have meaning and come from the lips not the heart. It is frequently only in times of crisis or personal drama that prayers take on the emotion and meaning with which they were originally imbued.

Only in their hour of need will many individuals beg for help, to rectify a situation that they cannot accept or solve themselves. Most have a very definite idea of how they want the Divine Creative Energy to intervene and what they want the outcome of that intervention to be. It is rare that they leave it to the Divine Creative Force to decide how that help is delivered. A list is presented; our blueprint for what we believe will be our deliverance. If the demands are not met in the way we envisaged, we may decide that prayer does not work, that the Divine Creative Energy is not listening or on our side, and indeed we were intended to suffer as punishment for previous misdeeds. Our own belief system is the catalyst that will either help or hinder our communication with the Divine Creative Force and essentially determine the level of assistance we receive.

Prayer is an exchange of energy and there is an energetic component to the act of prayer which will determine the outcome of our prayer. When we pray using words that are devoid of any energy or emotion they will have less energetic charge than those uttered with the power of emotion and faith. Faith fundamentally alters the vibrational signature of that communication between the individual and the Divine Creative Force so that it becomes more in line with the vibrational signature of the Universe. We are essentially requesting that the

Divine Creative Force intervene in our lives and hence in this free will world are giving permission for intervention and aid. We acknowledge that we are not sure of how to handle the circumstance we find ourselves in and now need help.

Many people on the whole do not stop to consider why things have turned out the way they have. What their role in the manifestation and materialization of the whole scenario has been. In some instances they may very well appear to be victims of circumstances as in the case of a sudden death, when they may find themselves coping with a situation that is genuinely outside their control; but in other situations they usually have had a hand in creating the crisis they find themselves in, either by something they did or did not do. They begin to wonder why the events that have occurred should have occurred, and why do bad things happen to some people and apparently not others.

Why doth sinner's ways prosper while disappointment all my endeavours end...

In this line, Gerard Manley Hopkins, a poet and Jesuit priest, gives us an insight into a popular viewpoint of the world, 'sinners' vs. 'good people' and his belief that sinners should be punished while good people should prosper. This is the view that many people hold and one in fact that has been encouraged by the various religious institutes over the years. The only thing that has changed is who or what is considered 'good' and 'bad'. We decide who is worthy of the Divine Creative Force's help and use our prayers to intercede on their behalf. In entering into judgment either of our own actions or those of others we often seek to either justify or condemn; neither position is in alignment with the idea that we are divine beings having an Earthly experience, and that from time to time we may inadvertently engineer a situation from which our soul will encounter its greatest experience and awareness can develop.

We do not regard these times in which we are challenged as situations to be fully experienced and through which we will grow. We are unwilling to consider that they may contain an intrinsic benefit or blessing. Our first thought is to remove ourselves from the situation as quickly as possible, and to return everything to how it was. We see ourselves as being victimized and seek to apportion blame and judgment. In some cases we look for the punishment of someone we may consider to have wronged us, and relish the idea that they are getting their just desserts as they have adopted a position or behaved in a manner that we have not approved of. In others we may seek clemency for ourselves when things are out of our control, our way of life is threatened or we have to cope with circumstances not of our choosing or to our liking. In such circumstances, there is no sense of 'good 'or 'bad', we just want help to change the odds in our favor.

So who or what is this 'outside' help? For some it is a benevolent father figure always there to help; for others it is a figure that is kind on occasion but equally vengeful or wrathful if upset. He or equally she may be seen as a judge who will act fairly. Others hold the idea of a divine presence, an energy that has no human qualities but will always act in a way that follows the inherent laws of the Universe. It makes right all wrongs, bringing balance to where there has been imbalance. This energy cannot be reasoned with, implored or pleaded with; it merely takes corrective action to restore balance regardless of who is involved. And there is another group for whom there is no 'outer force', who are wholly dependent on their own ingenuity and resources. You win some, you lose some, you do your best with the resources you have got and then you wait and see. There is no guilt, no recrimination, that is just how it is, that is life.

So given all of the above which group do you fit into? In times of crisis which one are you? In contemplating this you become aware of how you see the world, the belief system and judgments by which you operate and those beliefs you have inherited and integrated from your familial line, and to which as you have experienced life you may have added to or subtracted from. It is this belief system which determines how you live your life, what situations you create and how you manage all situations that you encounter. Some people have accepted their familial and/or religious beliefs totally and have adhered to them exclusively, even when it has not been easy to do so. They have lived their lives by those beliefs and will pass them on to their own children unchanged and unmodified. Others will hold some core beliefs but will have released or adapted others as current life experiences have dictated. This is what the majority of people do; hold on to what they consider the more important values while releasing others they consider less important or outdated. There are those who may be more radical, deciding their belief system and way of life bear no resemblance to that of their parents or siblings and so create something new, which is in direct contrast to their familial beliefs but suited to their individual needs.

The point is there is no right or wrong, only choices, and those choices come with responsibilities, one of which is the acceptance of the outcome of that choice. This can be a difficulty as sometimes the results of our choices may be totally different to the outcome we had in mind. We can find ourselves unwilling or unable to accept the consequences of the choice we have made. Our belief system has led us to a conclusion or situation that we do not like and we find ourselves trapped, unable to escape. It is then we can decide that we feel unable to cope with the position we find ourselves in and look for intervention from an outside source and begin to pray.

These events can vary, from the sudden and life threatening, such as being caught up in an act of nature like a hurricane, avalanche, or accident in which our very lives are in danger, to the more banal where as a result of the decisions we made over a period of time we find ourselves with our backs to the wall. In the case of natural disasters it can appear that we are victims of circumstances and have been 'caught out'. The Universe is a living energetic moving mass, it is changing constantly on a massive scale and sometimes we humans get in the way of these huge moves. When we are in tune with nature we, like animals, can read the signs of the movements coming and can remove ourselves to a safer location. However, many have lost their connection with nature and either are unaware of, or choose to ignore their inner knowing and so can find themselves in the path of the full force of nature. Some may at a conscious level choose to be in that location for the experience and excitement that such an episode produces, feeling they can cope with whatever comes; storm chasers and those who engage in extreme sports would be examples of individuals who put themselves in the path of nature to experience the 'high' that such activities engender.

Other situations can be less dramatic but nonetheless traumatic; you embark on a certain course of action, take certain decisions that release a series of events with consequences that you were not expecting, or thought you could manage. Then you can't and suddenly all your preordained ideas of how the situation is going to play out become unraveled and you find yourself gazing into the face of the unknown, the unforeseen. You become unsure of how to move forward and begin to doubt your own choices and ability. It is at this point that we often seek reassurance from someone or something else and turn to that 'other' energy which we recognize as being greater and more omnipotent than we humans, whatever name we use. We turn to ask for help in the situation we find ourselves in and it is at this point our 'faith' comes into play.

The strength of our faith will determine the response we receive. If we request help but have little faith that we will be helped or indeed deem ourselves unworthy of divine intervention, then we may find that we have created a self-fulfilling prophecy. We will be vibrationally incompatible with the solution that the Universe provides; in short the Universe will not be able to deliver help, as we will be unwilling to accept it. Our lack of faith in the request being answered ultimately affects the outcome of the appeal. In such instances the individuals can become frightened and alarmed repeating their prayers with greater fervor, sometimes beseeching, sometimes threatening, pleading, bartering, and while engaged in this internal drama are totally unaware of what is happening around them. They have become so fixated on the fear of not being helped or have such a rigid idea of how their aid must be delivered that any other solution presented is not recognized.

Expectation can cloud awareness preventing us from seeing what we already have, and the potential solutions available to us. If we become too attached to a particular outcome we may fail to see other opportunities that are being presented. As humans we are limited to and by the five senses and so we interpret the world we live in within these limitations, receiving only a small portion of what is a very big picture. When we focus on a desired outcome we are often seeking an immediate fix for an immediate problem. The Divine Creative Force does not have such limitations and so the solutions for our difficulties can often be of a more long-term nature as opposed to instant gratification that we humans have come to expect.

There is the story of the man whose home was in the path of the river which had burst its banks during the monsoon period. The man took refuge on the roof of his house and cried out to God for help to save his life. He was a very devout man and had no doubt that his life would be saved by God. Presently his neighbor came by in a boat and urged him to get in; the man declined saying that God was coming to save him. A little time later a fisherman passed by and told him get on the boat as there was no time to lose. The man declined again declaring that God had never let him down before, and he was sure he was on his way to save him. Finally as the man was perched on the very pinnacle of the roof, some survivors of the flood passed by on a makeshift raft and urged him to jump on before he was completely submerged and drowned. He politely refused, informing them that he was just waiting on God to arrive. The raft drifted on and the water levels rose until eventually the house was submerged and the man drowned.

When the man got to heaven he was none too pleased and said to God, "Why did you abandon me? I called on you to save me, why didn't you answer my prayers?" God replied, "But I did; I sent your neighbor to fetch you, the fisherman and the people on the raft but each time you refused to be saved." The moral of the tale being that help can come in unexpected ways, wrapped in surprising packages, so it is best to keep an open mind and be aware of any opportunity that offers a solution to the situation.

We are spiritual beings having a human experience and as such it is the soul that sets the agenda for the life we are to have, not the human 'ego'. The soul seeks to experience fully the emotional palette available in life here on Earth. It is not limited by the human desire to avoid pain, hardship and have a 'normal' limited life; it strives for growth through experience. Soul growth comes first; physical, mental or emotional discomfort is not a reason to avoid growth. That does not mean that consideration is not given to what is happening on the physical plane. Nothing will be done by the soul to deliberately injure the body on the physical plane, but neither will it allow personal discomfort to stop it experiencing all that life has to offer which includes what we have judged as the 'good, the bad and the ugly'.

The soul does not have these judgments. It is infinite and as such has no limits and fears nothing; it is open to experiencing everything. This is why it appears from our limited perspective that 'God' allows bad things to happen to good people. It is their soul that has sought that challenge, that experience. When these people are interviewed at a later date they will identify those crisis moments as the time their life changed irrevocably, when they gained a new insight, discovered something within them they did not know was there or made changes that improved their lives, their outlook or attitude.

It needs to be acknowledged that not all moments of crises result in life-changing moments. They have the potential to, but may not be realized as on Earth people have free will and are allowed to choose. Those involved may decide a particular decision or course of action is too hard, they can't do it and give up. They can refuse the opportunity to grow, preferring to stay with what they know or where they are. It may be due to a lack of faith in their own abilities, a lack of trust that they will be taken care of or at the behest of their ego which fears any change, but that is their choice. They will not be punished; rather another opportunity to develop will be presented at a later time. The soul will still keep challenging until eventually the experience is achieved; it may be within this lifetime or another. There are no constraints of time; the soul can take as long as is needed to complete this task. It is timeless; it is only the physical body that has a definite lifespan.

Prayer has a very important role in soul experience. It connects the human with the Divine and can help ensure that they are on a compatible vibrational frequency; when prayer is said from the heart that vibrational compatibility is guaranteed. It does not matter what words are said or where they are said; when they are said from the 'heart' they have true meaning and power. So often prayers become a duty, a ritual and are repeated as 'empty' with little thought and no connection with the heart.

Prayer comes with different levels of heart and it is this 'heart' that indicates the strength of our connection with the Divine Creative Force. When we pray from the heart that prayer travels faster and further into the Universe and is answered more readily than if we repeat strings of words to which we have no connection. It is often only in times of crisis that we allow the heart to open and allow ourselves to become vulnerable enough to feel the deep emotion that such crisis evokes. It is only when we are at our most 'alone' that we actually connect with the Divine Creative Force and discover that we are not alone, that we have a myriad of help there awaiting our call to galvanize its power to come to our aid. We also become aware that we are much more powerful beings than we realize, and have within gifts and attributes that we did not know we possessed.

When we detach ourselves from the hustle and bustle of daily living we become aware of an internal world that is the true source of our being and power. When we set aside time for 'prayer', meditation or quiet reflection, we find this inner world. In connecting with this inner world we can make sense of the outer world. This inner world gives us the stability and knowledge to cope with the chaos that we are encountering in the outer world. It is here we receive the answers as to what we need to do next, or how to resolve the situation that we find ourselves in.

While prayer is the request for help, meditation is the key to accessing the inner world where we can listen for the answer. It is while in this quiet space, when the conscious mind has stopped chattering, creating fear, anxiety and helplessness, that all is revealed, an idea, a course of action, a solution, something that will move the situation forward and allow us to experience the power of our own being. It inevitably means that we will have to take action and sometimes that action requires us to move out of our comfort zone and take a risk, but in that action is the experience that the soul seeks.

Meditation is regarded by some as one of the oldest forms of prayer and has been practiced for thousands of years by many of the Eastern religions and the Esoteric Schools of ancient times. It is at the heart of many of our modern-day religions and the means by which divine information was transmitted from the Divine Creative Force to the individual on Earth. It was while in meditation under a Bodhi tree that Buddha received the download that formed the teachings of modern-day Buddhism; and it was while in an altered state of meditation that Mohammed also received the teachings on which Islam is based.

Meditation is the practice of going within to connect directly with that aspect of our own divinity that is connected to the Divine Creative Force, and once connected we have at our disposal all the knowledge and wisdom of the Universe. It allows us to disconnect from the drama and the routine of the physical reality, and invites us into a vast space of awareness where nothing is judged, all is allowed and the heart is at peace. Mental and emotional stresses and struggles are set aside and in that moment there is a sense of having come home: nothing is expected, all is accepted and the soul is bathed in the light of unconditional love.

The road to achieving this state of what 'bliss' was, was the closely guarded secret of the chosen few; only those who dedicated their lives to its pursuit or practiced for many hours over many years were privileged to enter this state. There are tales of sages, Sadhus, monks and high priests who spent lifetimes perfecting the art of meditation, sitting motionless in Himalayan caves or locked up in high altitude monasteries far away from the humdrum of daily life. It is small wonder that with such mystery and intrigue there are many myths and legends surrounding meditation that lead many to believe that it is not for the ordinary person; that like the four-minute mile it takes years to perfect, and that it may not be within their capability to achieve.

There is also the supposition by some that you have to be 'holy' in order to meditate, and much has been made of the technique involved in meditating that for some it seems an insurmountable task. Nothing could be further from the truth; there are many paths to reaching this space of inner peace. There is not one any better than the other; there is only choice, choosing the technique that suits you best.

Meditation does not always involve sitting in a cross-legged position thinking no thoughts, as depicted in many Eastern portraits. It can be active meditation achieved through movement as in a walking meditation or as in Sufism through dancing to rhythmical music, usually drumming which increases in intensity and speed until the conscious mind can no longer hold control, and the dancer or the swirling dervish is transported to that state of euphoria where they enter the universal field of space and beyond. This ancient form of active meditation was practiced by many traditions in many continents as a means of crossing from the physical plane to what were regarded as the inner planes, where all could be revealed and communion with the Gods was possible.

However, there are less frenetic forms of active meditation if the swirling dervish does not appeal. These can include a peaceful walk through the park being aware of the colors in nature, the sights, the smells, the sounds, tuning into the beauty that surrounds you, being conscious of and paying attention to the details of what you are hearing, smelling, seeing, touching, and sensing the ambience of where you are. By increasing awareness of what you perceive you automatically tune into the vibrational frequency being emitted by each living thing be it plant, tree, water, rock, and are in communion with the Divine Creative Force as it is manifest in Nature. As there is no separation only oneness, by allowing the connection with Nature and hence the Divine you enter into that state of deep inner peace where nothing is judged and you are free to be who you truly be. Similarly in walking meditation by being consciously aware of how each foot is placed on the ground and the movement of the feet on the Earth, there is no room for any extraneous thoughts. The conscious mind is quieted and the connection to the inner voice can be established.

There are some meditative practices that use mantras or specific word combinations which are constantly repeated in order to gain access to the inner peace, and once again the aim is to distract or disconnect from the conscious mind and the conscious stream of thoughts and ideas that are being picked up and transmitted in to the mind. One of the simplest but equally effective methods of meditating is by following the course of the breath as it moves in and out of the body with the attention focused on breathing. Once again there is no room for wayward or intrusive thought forms to enter the consciousness. By inhaling for a particular number of breaths, holding for a specific number of seconds, and exhaling for a set number of seconds the mind is so fully engaged in the process it has no room for other thoughts and so the conscious mind is tricked into submission and access gained into the inner realms or sacred space.

For those who are more visually orientated, visualizations are an excellent means by which once again the chattering mind can be stilled. During visualizations the individual is asked to create an image or movie in the mind. It may involve going for a walk through nature noticing all the various aspects of the scene, or it may be moving through a building either from top to bottom or vice versa. It might even involve a journey using various forms of transport or a voyage out into galactic space. The stimulus does not matter, the effect is the same; for the time that the conscious mind is fully focused in creating visual images the attention is being guided into the sacred space, and all errant thought forms whether belonging to the individual or others are being disentangled from, and in the ensuing silence the connection with the higher self can be established.

As alluded to earlier there is now scientific evidence to indicate that we are energetic beings who act very much like transmitters picking up energetic thought forms and information. These thought forms can come from anywhere or from anyone and have been generated by others who are at a similar vibrational frequency to that which we emit, much like a radio station which transmits its sound waves on a particular wave band. Only by turning the dial to that specific wavelength do we 'tune in' to the station. In daily life this is occurring all the time, but we are very much oblivious to this fact and tend to assume that every thought we have is generated by us, so it is not surprising that we become overloaded with what can appear to be an unending stream of random information and thought forms which we then struggle to make sense of. This creates a lot of stress in the body as often we are not content with merely being aware of the thought; we then ascribe it meaning and emotion and so it becomes ours.

This explains why we can be driving along quite happily, and then for no apparent reason or without any provocation or justification we find ourselves in a rage. We may recognize if aware that we have no reason to be angry but more often we will pin that emotion onto some past experience that caused us anger and then we begin reliving the event or daydreaming another complete scenario with no basis in this reality. All that has happened is that we have tuned into someone else's rage and attributed it to ourselves. Meditation allows us to switch off this barrage of energetic garbage, which very often can be overwhelming, unrelenting and in some instances downright harmful to our own mental and emotional state. It provides a space where we can recharge our own batteries and in the silence take stock of where we are. It is often while in the meditative state that solutions appear, a knowing is gained and a sense of equilibrium established to the beleaguered mental, emotional and physical bodies.

The effects of meditation on the physical, mental and emotional well-being of the individual have been well documented. Scientific experiments carried out on yogis who meditated on a very regular basis proved that in this altered state blood pressure could be reduced and the heartbeat slowed down to a level that hither to had been thought impossible. It had always been assumed that the heart was outside the control of the individual, that there was a natural rhythm which while reacting to events within its environment e.g. beating faster after exercise or during stressful periods or slowing down when the body was at rest could not be voluntarily controlled by the individual. Experiments with the yogis proved that while in a meditative state these yogis could indeed control not only their heart rate but also their breathing patterns and the amount of oxygen they allowed into their bodies with no adverse effects.

Meditation also can alter the wave patterns in the brain and has a positive effect on both the mental and emotional state of the individual. By engaging in 20 minutes of meditation on a daily basis science has found that those involved have a more positive outlook on life, they are more at peace and feel better able to cope with the challenges that they meet. Meditation is yet another potent and free tool that we have within us which allows us to truly to become masters of our own lives.

Some may choose not to believe in a Divine Creative Force. They have put their 'faith' in the power of the intellect to respond to the situations that they meet. When problems are encountered or disappointments occur the response chosen is viewed as coming from logical reasoning and deductive thought. They have decided that as all problems are a product of logical thought processes, then the solutions needed are also to be found in that realm. The mind is regarded as the crucial determiner in arriving at conclusions, and any solutions engineered are within the confines of the conscious and subconscious mind. The implementation of these solutions may require the cooperation and assistance of other individuals or institutions and their willingness to participate. In some instances the individual may have to have 'faith' that they will do what they are asked or what they promised to do.

While this approach may work in certain situations, many are finding that of late this logical thought is not able to compete with all the uncertainties occurring on Earth at this time. It limits the options available, to prediction based on past experience, and removes the possibility of miracle and magic both of which are possible when the intervention of the Divine Creative Force is directly requested. The faith required when we invoke the aid of the Divine Creative Force is not a blind faith; rather it is an active faith that requires action coupled with an awareness of where and when a solution is presented. It is a faith based on partnership, for in oneness there is no hierarchy.

On Earth there have been so many instances where blind faith in another individual to take a course of action that we wish them to take, or make decisions that are in our best interest, or take care of something for us that we have placed value has led to disillusionment and harm. An astute salesman or well qualified professional or charismatic individual, who has promised financial security, complete health, enlightenment, or whatever the individual requests, has turned 'faith' into total reliance in which responsibility is abdicated. The individual moves from being the Divine Creative Force in their lives to being the victim at the whim of another; this is not faith but subservience. In making that choice a no choice position has been activated in which choice becomes limited; but the individual still bears responsibility for their life and the consequences of that choice.

As a divine being the person we should have 'blind faith' in is ourselves and not another. In connecting with our inner world we reveal the true meaning of the word love, not the definition projected on billboards and advertisements, but that unconditional love that comes from the heart and is the essence of who and what we are. When we discover and accept that this is so, then the crisis melts for we are sure of ourselves and accept that we are an integral, cherished part of the Universe. In this knowledge we find the safety and surety we need to walk fearlessly through the world and deal with whatever challenges come our way. We find the learning in every situation and the silver lining in every experience.

Faith and prayer are powerful tools in helping to uncover this but their power resides within us. It is the power we as individuals give them and that power comes from the amount of heart we put into them or rather allow into them and each of us has an infinite amount of heart to give. When we give this freely we energize our prayer and strengthen our connection with the Divine Creative Force. The answer to our prayer will come; it may not be in the form we have asked for or may be in a way that we were not expecting, but we have faith it will be answered in a way that will be for our highest good and ultimately promote soul growth through experience. Consider the following to develop Faith and Prayer...

- What do I need to be aware of here that may be a solution to my problem?
- What can I ask the Divine Creative Force for that will improve the situation?
- What blessing is contained within this situation that I am not aware of?
- What skills and talents have I got that would improve this situation?
- How can I use my breath to further strengthen the connection with my inner world?

Part 8

The Gift of Grace and Blessings

Grace is a term that has appeared in the doctrine of all the major religions of the world, including the various Christian, Islamic, Hebrew and Hindu texts. It is generally regarded as a 'God given' energy; a force that is totally empowering and comes from the creative source of the Universe; it cannot be earned by the efforts of man; it has to be bestowed on the individual by the Divine Creator or 'God'. The various doctrines would argue that Grace is given only to the 'good and virtuous' and that while it is 'God's' to give there is a better chance of receiving it if you adhere to the teachings of that particular doctrine.

In his book *Power vs. Force* Dr. David Hawkins defines Grace as being an aspect of enlightenment which he regards as "the peak of the evolution of consciousness in the human realm." In achieving enlightenment the individual has transcended the ego, there is no sense of self or duality, all has merged into oneness with the Divine. This ultimate state of being which is regarded in Eastern philosophy as 'Nirvana' is achieved only by the very few and the vision and teachings of such individuals can raise the collective awareness of all of humanity. Their teachings and vision are said to contain 'Grace' as they can create within the individual an infinite peace that goes beyond words. Such beings are said to be in a 'state of grace', that is the energetic level which they habitually inhabit. Individuals such as Jesus Christ, the Lord Buddha or Prophet Mohammed it is said all dwelt in this state of Grace.

Grace is essentially a state of 'oneness' with everything in the Universe, every star, planet, galaxy and life form. It is a state of 'being' not 'doing'; when we are in grace we are in complete communion with everything, there is no separation only oneness; there is no space or time only being fully and completely the divine being you really are. The majority of humans on Earth at this time do not live in this state of grace, their vibrational or energetic level is much different, but from time to time they do experience for a brief period 'grace' in their lives. This may be to cope with situations that are of themselves traumatic and painful when they have exhausted their own resources but somehow find the will, the energy to keep going through a particularly challenging or dark period in their lives. Many are not aware of it while in the crisis but on reflection identify it as a time when additional help was being given by a force greater than themselves, something outside themselves that guided and moved them through the crisis. Alternatively we have all experienced the 'Midas touch', when everything we decide to achieve is successful and it seems with only the minimum of effort on our part. We carry out tasks or actions in a Zen-like state with nothing causing difficulty and everything flowing naturally and effortlessly. So rare is this that we are immediately aware of it and identify a greater power than ourselves at work. In these circumstances we consider ourselves blessed to have received 'Grace' directly into our lives.

In both these situations people describe it as the 'hand of God' in events, and sense that there was something extra in the mixture that was not of their own making but which had a tremendous effect in assuring a positive outcome. For the time we are in this 'state of grace' our own creative energy and the creative force of the Universe are in perfect alignment hence our thoughts, ideas manifest and materialize effortlessly into our reality. We vibrate at the same vibrational frequency as the creative force of the Universe and as a result are 'in the flow' or 'the Zone'.

In its simplest form Grace can be seen as a pleasurable state of our highest being, as humans, where the attributes of kindness, beauty and optimism abound and we are in perfect alignment with the creative force within. Once received, Grace can be used to enhance our lives here on Earth, helping manifest that which is for our highest good. Grace creates a powerful, direct connection with the creative force of the Universe. This link can be activated by requesting it; when we ask for the gift of grace in our life we are requesting a form of Divine connection that has implicit in it an understanding that we will accept that which is for our 'highest good'. From our limited viewpoint we are not privy to what constitutes our 'highest good', as we see a limited aspect of the whole and so must trust that our highest good is being catered for, even though things turn out differently from how we imagined they would; that is why the virtues of acceptance, trust and non-judgment are also inherent in the gift of Grace.

The concept of Grace has occurred frequently in all the major religious texts and is often presented as yet another unobtainable virtue or substance given as a reward or withheld as punishment. Those born into the Christian faith have been told that they are born without Grace and that they enter this world 'in a state of sin'. This Original Sin that stains their soul has been inherited from the past behavior of 'Adam and Eve', who were made in the image of God and who as a result of disobeying God and eating the forbidden fruit were banished from the Garden of Eden to live out their lives on Earth in shame and despair. Humanity as their direct descendant carries this Original Sin. It never diminishes over time nor can it be avoided by any soul entering the Earth plane. It is the loss of the Grace of God that has resulted in the direct connection with God and the heavens being broken.

This, it is hypothesized, is one of the main reasons why life on Earth can be so difficult and the nature of humankind so predisposed towards 'sinfulness'; it is the absence of God's grace that makes it so, thus every Christian is given the concept that they are imperfect and indeed damaged. They are programmed with the idea of separation, unworthiness, imperfection and shame. They have been told their one role in this lifetime is to win back God's Grace, that they have one chance only to make amends and even then may not be successful unless they follow a prescribed set of doctrine as laid out by that particular church. And while the instructions and dogma may change it is similar with all religions. All encourage the belief of human imperfection, focusing on the shortcomings of humanity, while at the same time promising a 'cure' which comes in the form of a set of prescribed beliefs and doctrines embellished with rituals and ceremonies which must be rigidly adhered to if they wish to be saved and achieve 'eternal salvation', 'nirvana' or 'paradise'.

When we as a soul enter or incarnate into this world, it is by choice. We have come to experience that which our soul requires in order to develop, that it might truly express its love for and oneness with the Universal Creator. The fact that we have entered a physical density which is very far removed from the total energetic vibration of the Universe means we feel more isolated or separated from the Source or Divine Creator. It is not that we 'are' disconnected from the source, rather we 'feel' less connected, surrounded as we are by this denser energy. We cannot feel the 'at oneness' with the Divine Creator as easily as when we existed in the Universal plane. It is not that it is absent; rather we have to consciously 'tune in' more than we needed to do previously. We do this in a number of ways by going deep within ourselves through silence or meditation and reestablishing that connection with the Creator. Or by going into nature and experiencing the beauty that is around us and connecting with the energy that exists within all living things, for it is in this environment that the creative force of the Divine is most visible on the Earth plane. It is this latter path that all the ancient peoples on Earth have used, from the Native Americans to the Aborigines to the Bushmen of the Kalahari; all connected with the Great Spirit by communing with Nature.

Once we make it our intention to connect with the Divine Creator the rest is carried out for us. Some souls upon reaching Earth 'forget' to 'tune in' and this can increase their sense of isolation, they get caught up in the need to survive and the dramas of living, forgetting that there is another world to which they have access, and if entered would help them create the life that they want. Some individuals are aware of this 'other world' but they have been programmed to accept their unworthiness and imperfection and so often feel they have no right to seek connection, afraid that their lowliness would be an obstacle to their being accepted and so they do not even try, expecting rejection.

But there is every reason to tune in, for once we become aware that Grace is freely and abundantly available to all who ask and that by invoking this energy a power is released which will change our outlook and attitude to life allowing us to make life-affirming changes, we begin to feel less alone in life and have a sense that we are being cared for, that we matter and have a sense of belonging. We realize that we have not been abandoned to fend for ourselves. We are part of the Universe and at one with everything in it. We have at our disposal the resources of that universe and can tap into those resources any time we choose. We do not need to earn that right nor is it dependent on age, gender, education or religion. It is our birthright; we need only to ask. To use a familiar analogy it is like being on an island where in one scenario you have a direct link to a cargo ship that supplies all your needs, gives you advice and information on the situations you are encountering; in the second scenario being on a island with no form of communication with the outside world and trying to make the best of and interpret the situations and experiences you are meeting. These situations would engender completely different responses and evoke an entirely different set of emotions, behaviors and attitudes.

In the initial situation the only thing that could possibly

interrupt the line of supply would be if we sent mixed messages about what we wanted, or decided halfway through that we did not want what we had asked for and changed our mind, which is our right under the gift of free will. Then supplies could get delayed or be returned to the ship to await new orders.

When you feel you have a connection with or to something there is a greater sense of ease, and contentment. It allows you to be more adventurous and courageous than if you feel alone, unsupported, with no one to listen to your concerns, help you solve or at least make sense of all the experiences you encounter. This then is the role of Grace, an energy that can be tapped into on a daily basis in your life. It is the lifeline issuing directly from the Creator that will help you achieve your needs, goals and desires, the means by which you can take various circumstances and by requesting Grace transform those situations into something they previously were not.

The invocation may be that with Grace the situation be resolved, that a solution is presented that you had not considered or that you find within yourself some particular quality that hitherto you felt was missing or greatly reduced in your character, or it may be that you just find within yourself the courage to take a particular course of action. Whatever the request, by asking for the gift of Grace from the Universe, you are essentially asking to be aligned with the creative force and energy of the Divine.

Grace is essentially the Creator's love manifest in energetic form that allows us to accomplish something that would not be possible with our own limited beliefs in our energetic resources. By invoking Grace in our daily lives we gain access to that endless source of universal energy to transform any situation. The only thing we must be conscious of in invoking Grace that as it comes directly from the Creator and is composed entirely of the vibration of love; it cannot be summoned to harm or hurt another. It can only be used to resolve situations or enhance our energy that we might achieve our highest good, and serves the highest good of all those concerned.

It is this last proviso that has confused humankind and many will claim that Grace has not been received or been withheld as a punishment because a desired outcome has not been achieved, an enemy has not been smote, a specific resolution not achieved as requested.

Grace has its basis in love and responds best to those requests which have their basis in love with a strong intention based in the desire to grow and recognize the divine being that we truly are. It is not a prize to be won or lost, nor a reward or punishment. It is an ever-present energy that is freely and abundantly given, it is yours for the asking. It is energy based in love and of love, and eagerly responds to any request that comes from an open heart, clarity of intention that involves the desire to improve, grow, resolve and evolve. Too often this has not been the case and the 'Grace of God' has been summoned to administer Divine retribution on those perceived to have done wrong or where it is felt an injustice has occurred; but just as a loving parent will not give one child a stick so he can beat his brother, neither will Grace be granted to another as a means of gaining domination or to mete out punishment.

Grace can only be activated by love but once activated there is no measure or restriction placed on it. It is wholly given and strengthens both the requestor and the situation it is applied to so that a speedy peaceful resolution can be achieved, one that is for the highest good of all concerned. Once invoked be assured that all is being taken care of; have no expectations as to the outcome, your needs will be met in a manner that as yet you may not have considered never mind hoped for. Sometimes you may see a resolution, other times not; but the invocation has not been lost or misheard. The work has occurred behind the scenes and you will be shown the results in due course.

Grace can be requested at any time but it will also be

provided by the Divine Creator when it is deemed that it can be used at that particular point in time to meet a challenge or move into the next stage of soul growth. From our limited viewpoint here on Earth it can seem that its appearance in our life is arbitrary and at the whim of the Divine Creator, but in fact it is quite the opposite. It comes at a time when we need it most or at a point when we can make best use of it to grow.

Blessings are another form of energy that we can and do invoke frequently in daily life both for our own personal use and to be given as a gift by us to others. To bless another is to request that the grace of God be visited upon that individual with the express intention that it will benefit them. In blessing another person, object, or event we are adding energy to that which we have blessed. We are asking the Universe to pour additional energy into that situation so that it may become more or better than it is at present. We can bless all sorts of things – the food we eat, the water we drink. Science has now proved that the vibrational energy of that which we bless increases following that blessing.

The same principle applies when we bless situations, people, events; we change the vibrational frequency by the addition of universal energy so that its potency is increased and the possibility of a favorable outcome more likely. We are energetic beings and are constantly receiving signals from our environment both at a conscious and unconscious level. While we may not always be consciously aware of being blessed, we are aware on an energetic level that something has changed. We may not be able to put words on it but we are aware when someone thinks well of us and wants us to succeed or to be the best we can.

The idea of Blessings has been around for centuries and is part of our language and culture. We say 'Bless you' when someone sneezes, conferring upon them extra energy to ensure good health. We can also use 'Bless you' as a form of thanks for an unexpected kindness or help spontaneously given. We use it to describe someone who has experienced favorable circumstance with the words 'They were blessed' or referring to a situation that might have had an unhappy ending but for divine intervention 'We were blessed'. We 'bless' food before eating to give thanks for its presence and the meal that we are sharing with others.

In past times there was an awareness of the role of blessings in daily life; people were greeted with a blessing and leave taken with a blessing. Blessings were automatically spoken upon entering a house, before accepting food, on hearing good news and families were blessed before undertaking any journey. In our modern world the art of blessing another is practiced by the few but we still appreciate being blessed as we recognize the surge of love we get from such a practice.

Blessings, like Grace, is love made manifest in energetic form and bestowed from the heart of one person onto another, with the prime purpose of bettering that individual's life. It comes from the heart, is instantaneous and abundant. It not only benefits the receiver but also the giver, as in creating that blessing the heart opens to the energy of the Universe and we have the opportunity to become that which we truly are: Love Incarnate. Consider the following to activate Grace and Blessings daily...

- On what challenge in my life do I request the presence of Grace to bring it to a Divine resolution? (Make the request.)
- In what area of my life do I require Grace and Blessing? (Make the request.)
- Who requires Grace & Blessing in their lives today?
- Where can I direct Grace & Blessings today that will benefit both the Earth and all of humankind?

Part 9

The Triad of Intuition, Discernment and Trust

We are born on to this planet as creations of Divinity that have come to have a physical experience, and as such we arrive with many inherent abilities and talents that it is hoped during this current lifetime we will become aware of, develop, and use to help smooth the transition from the non-physical to the physical. These abilities are actually gifts from the Divine Creative Force designed to help us navigate our way through the non-familiar environment of duality, polarity and illusion, and as with any gift it is our choice whether to accept or reject it.

One particular triad of gifts at our disposal to help in the navigation through the constant barrage of information and dramas that we experience in this ever-changing environment are those of intuition, discernment and trust. The awareness and use of these three qualities can determine the manner in which our life unfolds as they contain within them a level of consciousness that will fundamentally color how we operate in this time-space continuum.

Each of these qualities are independent and can be used as such; however, when used together their combined effect surpasses anything that can be achieved individually. When we develop intuition without trust, we will be unsure if what we are intuiting is correct or not. Concerned that we are deluding ourselves and that our intuition is a figment of imagination reflecting our mind's desire as opposed to a communication from our higher self, it is unlikely that we will have much faith in the messages received and will look to outward sources for answers. Once we do that we are very much at the mercy of the opinions of others and their prejudices, which may not always be in our best interests. We may not even trust the advice given and spend our lives in a heightened state of anxiety agonizing over every decision and always unsure whether the choices we made were right or not.

Similarly if we don't develop discernment we accept everything, whether good or bad, and once again are easily influenced by outside forces that will have their own agenda and may encourage us to take action or accept beliefs that are limiting, and prevent us from realizing our true potential. We can end up living our lives according to the dictum of others and not our own truth. This has repercussions as there will always be a nagging suspicion that there is more to life than we are currently experiencing, and yet we cannot seem to put our finger on what it is that is missing. We may seek that fulfillment in the material world – if I had a new car or was a millionaire or had a new relationship or a family then everything would be fine. However, even when we achieve the material goals we set or the items we desire, the sense of gratification or satisfaction is short-lived and it is not long before the same feeling of 'something missing' returns.

Our higher self, that aspect of our being that is in direct contact with the Divine Creative Force, will not accept the limitations that it is being held under, and will always seek new and novel ways to make life on Earth meaningful and to awaken the individual to its presence; but without the development of Intuition, Discernment and Trust its job is much more difficult and we can remain unaware of our own Divinity over our complete lifetime.

As infants when we arrive on Earth it is generally assumed that we are helpless. This is true on the physical level; we are born in need of food, warmth, and have very limited physical movement. However, we are born with a natural 'instinct' for survival and it is this that is automatically triggered when we emerge into our new world. This is reflected in the first cries of the infant which initiates a reaction in those adults around it to protect, nourish and take care of the newborn. This adult reaction referred to as the 'maternal instinct' can be observed not only in the human species, but also in the animal kingdom and includes many species from whales and apes to elephants and birds to name but a few. The duration of the maternal instinct varies from species to species, but is basically active until the young are able to take care of themselves. In the human species this is usually a lifelong feeling and is deemed as part of the nature of human beings, particularly the female of the species.

Instinct remains with us throughout our lives although its strength will vary from individual to individual, and also from circumstance to circumstance. The soldier in the war zone will have a stronger survival instinct than the individual sitting at home watching TV. Instinct is essentially self-preservation, and is a set of primal impulses that are there to ensure the survival of the individual. It has four basic goals: to preserve life, avoid death, procreate and have adequate sustenance for the body. Instinct is not the sole preserve of human beings; it can be observed in all living species on Earth at this time. It is 'instinct' that alerts the species to the changes that need to be made either in action or reaction to circumstances in order to survive.

It is argued in humans that natural or basic instinct is under the control of the 'ego' which has been described as "the core around which the personality is built," by Sathya Sai Baba; or alternatively as a subjective feeling by which the individual identifies 'What I am, what is me and mine'. Ego is essentially a fear-based consciousness which strives to maintain control through gratification of the senses. Instinct as directed by ego relates primarily to survival in the physical world and negotiating the environments in which we find ourselves, through analysis of the thousands of pieces of sensory information that we receive on an ongoing basis; but we humans have another tool which we are gifted with on our arrival on the planet. Once our basic survival is assured, it is the ability to 'intuit' from which intuition develops.

Intuition operates on a different level from instinct and is the direct link we have to our higher self or soul. It is often described as the inner voice which seeks to guide us in our daily life, helps us resolve problems and make decisions that are in our best interest, and alerts us to when all is not as it seems. It is the means by which we can navigate all the challenges and obstacles that we encounter on our journey in this world. Intuition as a concept has over the centuries lost its former importance and value. While once revered as the individual's link with divinity, it has become disrespected and a source of derisory comment.

Individuals who had developed their intuitive abilities were in past times honored for their knowledge and wisdom. However, the misuse of this gift and attempts by some to use their intuitive abilities to control others and even predict future events eventually led to it being seen as solely manipulative or fraudulent. Demands were made for proof of its existence which could not be done within the limited scope of scientific research in its present form – limited as it is to the investigation of physical matter. The scientists could not prove its existence; therefore for many this became conclusive evidence that it did not exist. Over time its development and use were actively discouraged, linked as it was with the occult and 'supernatural forces'. It was portrayed not as something that was part of the human consciousness but rather a force outside the individual; those who had strong intuition or developed it in any way were regarded with suspicion, often being labeled as being 'in league with the devil' and were punished accordingly. There was little incentive to strengthen the bonds between the individual and their intuitive abilities, and over successive generations intuition as a life guidance tool dissipated; very few people openly discussed its existence. It became thought of as a gift given to the special few rather than something inherent in every person, there to be developed and used.

At present the connection between individuals and their intuition is weak. In some cases it fails to operate, either through underuse or ignorance of its existence. So what is the role of intuition? Do we need it and can we trust it? Intuition in its purest form is our direct means of communicating with the soul or higher self, as the soul is one with the Divine Creative Force and all the information held therein. It is a means of communicating with the Divine Creative Force in a more direct way. It is a two-way communication system, in which we can ask for help, solutions or advice on any topic or event and receive feedback. We look within to find the answers. It sounds so simple we may ask: why don't we automatically use this tool? The answer is equally simple: in order to access our intuition we must first calm the 'chattering mind' or as it has been referred to the 'monkey mind', leaping rapidly from thought to thought, and this is where we often become ensnared.

The intuitive voice has been described as a quiet, peaceful voice heard when the mind is silenced. It is accompanied by a feeling of knowingness that, yes, this is the correct course of action, the correct answer or solution. In order to experience that voice we have to still the mind and this can be very difficult to do particularly as we have not been taught how to do this. We have been told about the power of the mind but we have not been taught about the power of our intuition. The mind operates on logical thought and like a computer it relies on what it is being fed to make a decision; all the individual's information, worldly knowledge and experiences are fed in, and then using just that information the mind formulates thoughts, ideas, creates solutions, or makes plans.

Intuition operates differently. It takes not only the information stored in the mind but it has also access to the knowledge and wisdom stored in the Divine Creative Force; and because it uses a different set of paradigms and is not limited by logical thought the solutions it has are better suited and correct for us. As Intuition has access to the whole picture, it is not limited by the constraints of human perception, logical reasoning or linear time thus the solutions it creates are more inventive, creative and take a long-term view as opposed to being a short-term fix. It has always at its core the highest good of the individual.

It has become very popular for people to be asked to 'think outside the box'; in fact many employers value it as a very definite asset in a candidate's resume. But what does that actually mean? It essentially refers to the ability to move past logical thinking, and whether they realize it or not those individuals who regularly practice this skill are in fact communing with their intuition, accessing 'universal or divine inspiration' and intuitive thought.

The link with our own personal intuition can be strengthened through use and belief in the accuracy of its responses. As we learn to respect, trust and act on our intuition these messages that come via the subconscious become stronger and more detailed. The subconscious becomes aware that it is being listened to, and takes a more active role in our lives. Using our intuition is one of the surest ways of being aware of and creating the right action in our lives. It is the means by which we can create and hold a direct connection with our soul and indeed the Divine Creative Force. By using it regularly it becomes a means through which we can banish any feelings of isolation and the belief that we are on our own with all our 'problems'.

In accepting that we have at our disposal a means of solving dilemmas our anxiety levels drop and we begin to relax, knowing that the responsibility for the decision-making process is shared. Intuition allows us access to the Divine Creative Force reminding us where we came from and where our true self really lies. It puts in perspective the many trials, tribulations and difficulties of everyday life, giving a spiritual dimension and offering a spiritual solution to all the challenges we encounter.

In this time of change it seems that there is no shortage of challenges, problems, or crises. We appear to move swiftly from one to the next without ever receiving a break. This can be exhausting if all we have on our side as an ally and confidante is mind. The logical mind can be a fickle ally linked as it is to emotion and ego. These two factors often influence its decision-making abilities and cause the pendulum to swing wildly back and forth depending on the emotion being felt at that particular time or how strongly the ego feels threatened, as the ego favors decisions that will prevent the loss of face or ones that minimize disruption to the individual.

It is little wonder that we often feel unsure in our ability to find solutions or are equally unsure in our choice. The logical mind often chooses short-term gain but this can lead to long-term pain. Intuition on the other hand has at the center of its being the highest good of all those involved, therefore the decision it leads us to ensures no harm is done to anyone involved in the situation and this prevents further long-term damage, recognizing as it does the 'oneness' that we all are.

So how can we access and revive this intuition? What must we do to have intuition as part of our daily decision-making process? Essentially we need to 'do' very little apart from make it our intention to reach a solution that is for the highest good of all those involved. In declaring this intention we immediately shift our focus into alignment with our intuition. We signal that we are allowing our intuition to become functional in our life and the stage has been set, the lines of communication have been opened for help with the problem or situation we find ourselves in. If we are unsure of whether we are indeed in contact with our intuition, we may need to reacquaint ourselves with the inner voice so that we can recognize it when we hear it.

To make that initial connection we travel within on the in-breath. By focusing on the breath we find a way to sidestep the various thoughts and ideas generated by the mind which can distract and entrap us. If the mind is consciously focusing on the breath it has no time to create thoughts or distractions, and soon we come to a place of stillness, quietness, and our 'sacred heart'. There is a peace which fills us and allows us to know we are home. As we stay there we become aware of a gentle voice which may ask us to listen, we may receive information regarding our current situation, insights as to why things have occurred or immediate solutions to problems. The answers can manifest in various forms; even if we are not given a definite solution we may perhaps later 'accidentally' meet someone who can be helpful to us, overhear, read or see something on the radio or TV which helps.

The Divine Creative Force is nothing if not inventive in delivering a solution to us, but we must be aware of and be open to receiving the answer to our question in an unorthodox manner. We have all experienced that gut feeling that strongly pushes us towards one course of action or repels us from another. That physical reaction is our intuition revealing itself, communicating its response that tells us this is or is not right for us. As we become more in tune with our intuition we become more aware of the fact that our intuition is constantly communicating with us, and many of these messages are nonverbally communicated through our body as physical reactions or vague feelings that we are often not quite sure how to interpret.

We have all been in situations where we have felt that everything is not as it appears and have had a physical response to that situation or an individual person. These may include: hairs standing on the skin, sudden changes in body temperature or a change in heart rate. There may be nothing visible to the naked eye that would warrant such changes yet we are experiencing them. Intuition is communicating with us but often we are so unskilled in decoding the message we fail to correctly understand its meaning. With practice we become more aware of not only when we are being contacted but what we are being told.

We develop a new relationship with our intuition, one in which we actively look to our intuition for help and guidance in all situations. As we begin to rely more on intuition for cues and responses to all we encounter on our journey through this Earth a wonderful thing happens, we move more with the flow. We react to situations more positively, more resolutely, spending less time working out the pros and cons, and more on 'being' and dealing with that situation.

In becoming more decisive, situations or people which previously would have engendered much angst, anxiety and worry disappear off our radar so the molehills never become mountains. In fact the landscape of our lives becomes much more undulating and passable than previously. Intuition provides us with a navigation system through life, one which does not rely on education, intelligence or social background to work. Everyone is born with intuition and each person has the same potential, the only thing that differentiates us is how aware we are of it and whether we use it. Many people will go through life unaware of its existence, while for others it is the barometer by which they live their lives and the means by which they create a life of their own choosing. You need no one's permission to use it but once aware of it you begin to ask 'What is my intuition telling me in this situation?', then you have begun the journey of opening up. Using intuition allows us to meet life's challenges in a more decisive manner and create the wonderful abundant peaceful and peace-loving life that we truly deserve.

Discernment as it is used in the worldly sense is the ability to make a selective judgment on information given, or in a situation encountered. It is the capacity to decide if the truth is being spoken, if a situation is one to become involved in or if a person is what they say they are. In spiritual terms, however, it is regarded slightly differently as there is a further consideration. Discernment in the spiritual sense is the ability to make choices as a consequence of paying close and particular attention to intuition. As discussed earlier, 'Intuition' has a vital role in guiding us through the situations, challenges and choices we may meet in life. Once we still our minds and listen to that quiet inner voice, we have connected with our intuition, and by putting into practice the advice and wisdom we receive from our intuition we then practice discernment.

We are being constantly bombarded with so much information that it is easy to become overwhelmed as there are so many companies, industries, governments trying to manipulate, cajole and persuade us into following their way of thinking. They want us to buy their product, adopt their policies or agree with their demands. It can be difficult to know what to do for the best, as not all have our best interest at heart. These companies or institutions are not aware of you as an individual or what your needs or wishes are; but based on a profile of tick boxes which they assume you will fit into, they think they know you and can predict your behaviors, buying patterns or future needs. Their sole purpose in gaining this information is rarely to give you the life you desire but rather to control and manipulate your beliefs, thoughts or money, while quietly disempowering you in the process.

Over the years decision-making has been actively discouraged; we have been encouraged to leave it to the 'experts' who know what they are doing. We have been assured that some things are much too complicated for us to have either an opinion or an idea on what needs to be done. Bureaucracy has flourished and become so convoluted and expansive that it has now become impossible for the mere mortal to navigate their way through all the various systems operating. Many people don't ever question, rather they look to those whom they think know better to give them the answers, or in other words to tell them what to do. The Internet has brought this into sharp focus as we are no longer presented with just one or two points of view on a subject; now we have instant access to hundreds of thousands of viewpoints on all topics and these views can be diametrically opposed. So how do we know which to trust or which viewpoint is right? How can we be assured we are making the decision that is right for us?

It is at this point that we need to begin to use the divine gift of discernment. It has been present within us all since birth and merely awaits activation. It is at its most potent when used with intuition and trust; it will with use become sharper, more immediate and totally accurate. But first we must become aware of it, use it and learn to trust it. Discernment is different to judgment in that it does not rely on ego, emotion and the logical mind; it goes directly to our intuition and listens to that. Too often our judgments are based on ego and emotion and rely on our belief system, life experiences and prejudices to come to a conclusion, using the logical mind as a sifter. This means the quality of the judgments we make can vary depending on what particular prejudice or belief we view the facts through, and the emotional state we are experiencing at the time.

It means also that we are open to manipulation through our emotions, and can be led into making choices that are not right for us. It is a tactic that has been employed over many millennia by those seeking to control or influence thinking. We usually are unaware of being manipulated, as the 'facts' being presented are usually so convincing and when coupled with an inbuilt 'fear and doubt' factor e.g. 'Can you afford to not to do this?', 'Are you sure you don't need…?' or 'This too could happen to you unless…' We feel compelled to act in the way suggested. This invariably leads to us making 'good' judgments which essentially means we can live with the consequences, and 'bad' judgments where the outcomes are not to our liking and have begun a chain of events that we are unable or unwilling to accept. This inconsistency has caused us to lose trust in our ability to make decisions with the result that when we do there is always an air of uncertainty as to whether we have made the right call or whether we have all the facts, or indeed been duped by others.

With discernment there is no judgment, merely an inner 'knowing' of what we need to do for our own highest good. There is no conflict of ideas; no weighing up the pros and cons and then agonizing over a decision or being at the mercy of the manipulation of others. There is grasping all the relevant ideas and then while listening to our inner voice we experience a 'knowing' of what the right course of action is and then taking it. Discernment allows us to see through the lies, the spin, the emotional manipulation. It lets us know that even when the logical mind is trying to take us down a road that sounds right, there is a feeling that signals that all is not well, that the whole truth is not being disclosed. In the early stages of using discernment we may not be able to put words on that uneasiness, but with practice and use we quickly learn to identify the issue.

As we have evolved as a species our faculty for discernment has become weakened. We do not have the strong sense of discernment that our forefathers had. We have become distracted by what is occurring outside ourselves and are constantly reacting to images, impressions, information that is being given to us at an ever-increasing rate. The increase in both volume and rate of information, not to mention the fact that many demand an instant response, has meant that we have not been aware of, or taken the time to use discernment in our decision-making process. In fact we often do not check in with ourselves to see what is or feels right or correct for us. We respond to the loudest, brightest stimuli as we continue to search outside of ourselves for our needs. We have lost a sense of that inner voice; or if we have chanced upon it we often ignore it, preferring as we do the answers given to us by the outside world. Our discernment has become diluted and underused as a result.

At this point in our lives we have little idea of how to use discernment; we allow others to convince us what is best for us and then become upset when the solution chosen does not fit our specific needs or is wrong for our own growth and development. We can at any point we choose reignite the lost art of discernment simply by taking time to ask ourselves the following questions when required to make a choice or decision. Is this right for me? Will this course of action be for my highest good? Or by directly looking to our intuition for guidance, 'Please guide me in the decision I need to make', and then waiting for the response. The response comes via the subconscious, and the language of the subconscious is not always in the form of words. It may come as a distinct feeling, a definite 'knowing', or we may gain access to further information which clarifies the situation, enabling us to act with confidence and certainty. The main point is you will be answered but need to be aware of the signals.

Our intuition is constantly communicating with us via the subconscious but many are unaware of the messages being given and as a result can keep making the same choices, which do not allow us to live a life of our choosing. We can, however, break this pattern by acknowledging that we have this gift within ourselves waiting to be developed and used. Once we do that we awaken our awareness and open a direct link of communication with our intuition. We can also discover the patterns of behavior and beliefs that have been preventing us from choosing courses of action that would have enabled us to have the life that we desire. In using discernment we begin to evaluate information in a very different way; no longer do we accept everything presented to us as fact just because it is being given by an 'authority'. We 'know' when we are being misled or when there is another agenda being served. The power of discernment gives us back a sense of power. No longer are we victims in this world; we are co-creators and can choose what to accept in to our belief systems and what to refuse.

What prevents us from practicing discernment? What holds many back is a lack of belief in ourselves and as a result of that – fear. We cannot accept that we have this direct link to the Divine

Creative Force, that we are so cherished and loved by the Creator that we have been given access to all the 'information' we will ever need to navigate our way fearlessly through the physical world. From birth we have received a lot of misinformation about who we are and what we are capable of.

These falsehoods have come from many sources but all have had the effect of causing us to doubt our own abilities and have made us afraid. We fear making a mistake, fear being taken advantage of, fear failure or of being seen as a failure. This belief in ourselves as failures or potential failures is one of the main reasons that we then distrust ourselves and, because we do not fully trust ourselves, naturally we do not trust ourselves to make good decisions and so we look to others to make decisions for us. In this way we abdicate ourselves from the responsibility of failure; after all we cannot be blamed if we were only following someone else's advice.

We refuse to believe that by connecting with our intuition we have a foolproof way of protecting ourselves from the manipulation of others. We do not believe that we could ever reach a position where we are totally comfortable with all the decisions we make, secure in the knowledge that we are being taken care of. We have been told that the world is a dangerous place and that we are on our own. We do not believe that we have all the help of the Divine Creative Force at our disposal to guide and protect us. In some cases we believe that we are beyond help and that only by reacting defensively can we protect ourselves from 'bad' things happening. In adopting this attitude we immediately close ourselves off to all the unseen help that is available. We rush into decisions and actions that do not honor us or reflect that which we wish to create in our lives. We 'react to' situations and circumstances as opposed to 'act on' them.

Decisions made with this mindset are more likely to have their base in fear and as such will not have our highest good in mind. We have not given ourselves a chance to act with discernment and have not allowed ourselves to listen to the inner voice which urges patience, caution or suggests a particular course of action. We react to situations because something within us identifies the similarities between the present event we are encountering and a past occurrence. Something about our current situation triggers a memory of an earlier experience causing us to seek a speedy conclusion to this event. We may be trying to avoid what has happened before if it was a negative experience, or indeed emulate what happened previously if it was a good situation. The point is we have not stopped long enough to use our discernment and find the correct solution in this 'here and now'.

More demands are being made on us to choose quickly. These choices have consequences and often we have little time to deliberate or confer with others on what is the right course of action for us. The truthfulness of the information we are being presented with can also be dubious, as all have their own agenda which may or may not have our best interest at heart. This can increase our sense of isolation and aloneness as we wonder who or what to trust. Discernment is a tool that can help us overcome these doubts and concerns. It reconnects us with the world by increasing our certainty in the decisions we make and allows us to reclaim our power, making it more difficult for others to manipulate or panic us into the wrong course of action. It is a direct link with the Divine Creative Force and is another treasure that lies within us waiting for discovery and use. Through use of discernment we learn to trust ourselves and to trust that we are being guided by a creator that only wants the very best for us. In using discernment in a conscious and constant way we build up our own wisdom.

Trust is the third aspect of the triad with intuition and discernment. It is a connection that is formed between two or more individuals or indeed with the self. It develops through practicing discernment in all situations and with all people. In its purest form Trust has its basis in unconditional love which is very different from the notion of romantic love that we all tend to immediately think of when we hear the word 'love'. Unconditional love is the purest and highest form of love that we can ever experience as humans. There are no conditions or restrictions in unconditional love, only recognition of the spiritual being within and the connection between all things. It recognizes that as we are all one with the Divine Creative Force, there is no separation only integration. Without this love there is no trust and without trust there is no love – they are inextricably linked.

Trust has at its foundation a basic desire for integration, and through this a creation of something new and improved. This may be an improvement in circumstances, situations, or a strengthening of the bonds between individuals. When we build trust with the self, this union leads to an increase in self-esteem, self-acceptance and self-love, all of which improve our ability to create a life of our own choosing. As trust grows, so does love, and equally as it diminishes so too can love. Trust is something that needs nurturing in order for it to develop. Once broken, it can be difficult to repair, not impossible, but it takes dedication, commitment, forgiveness and love to reinstate it. The concept of trust as it occurs in our current culture is less related to discernment and intuition and is more aligned with judgment than unconditional love.

A newborn has total trust as it does not have judgment, only an acceptance of the situation it finds itself in. It has an inherent trust that it will be cared for and nurtured by those adults around, and this is what adds to its vulnerability and innocence. As children we are developing life experience and trust our parents to make decisions for us that will keep us safe, fed, clothed and make choices that will be in our best interest. This is what happens for the most part but not always, and children through their lack of experience will accept most situations as 'normal'. However, as children develop thought and begin to use discernment as a means of deciding who or what can be trusted, they come to the conclusion that not all people or situations merit their total trust.

These basic attempts at using discernment are often overridden by well-meaning adults and societal norms, who consider it to be their role to make decisions for the child regarding it as has having neither the experience nor ability to do so. Children then begin to doubt their own ability to discern and rely more on the judgment of the parent or adult around them. They stop looking within and are taught to rely solely on their five senses and prior experience to 'judge' if a situation or person is trustworthy; their discernment becomes underused or never fully develops. At this point the first seeds of self-doubt and distrust develop.

Judgment by its very nature creates segregation and separation which is the antithesis of trust. As we travel through life we add to our life experience, our judgments grow, we meet people from all walks of life in a variety of situations and the level of trust that we give out is measured and very much linked to the judgment of that situation or person. We justify this position by claiming that trust can be broken. It can happen from very early on in our life when our parents' ability to nurture and love us in the way that we wanted was not met or when our trust in a beloved partner was shattered by either an action or a failure to act. We become more wary of people and situations, unsure of our own judgment, and as a result will not risk trusting out of fear that we might be 'misplacing' our trust.

When trust is linked solely to judgment there is always the possibility of disappointment. In judging others we close down our awareness of the oneness within life and see only the differences. It colors the way in which we view the world and the decisions we make as a result. When we examine the circumstances wherein our trust was 'broken', we often discover it was not so much that what we call our 'trust' was affected as our 'expectations' were not met in the way that we anticipated and as a result we are no longer sure of our ability to 'judge' people or situations, and this uncertainty causes us to feel unsafe and fearful.

Our modern society is full of people who have become damaged in the process of life and now operate outside the universal or spiritual laws, and so our trust has become conditional. We constantly assess and make judgments as to whom we share our trust with, measuring it out to ensure we are not duped or hurt. Our life experience has taught us it is not safe to give total trust, that we must always hold just a little back in reserve so that if something does go wrong or some event does not meet our expectations we have a 'get out' clause and can protect ourselves. We have been taught that we do not always get things to happen the way that we want them to, or that people will not always behave in the way we expect them to or wish them to, and so there is always the possibility of 'failure'.

These attitudes and beliefs formed on the Earth plane are then transferred to the Divine Creative Force and will reflect the level of trust that we are willing to risk in that particular relationship. We have concluded that the Divine Creative Force cannot be trusted to provide us with what we need, and ascribe to the Divine Creative Force the qualities that we have found in our fellow humans.

Our trust is often based solely on whether our expectations have been met, rarely acknowledging or recognizing that in those times, when it appeared we did not get what we wanted, we received something better which was of infinitely more value than what we had initially asked for, and served our highest good. We now have so little trust in our own requests being answered many feel the need for an intermediary to intercede on our behalf. As we pray or meditate to a particular deity we are asking and imploring their help in a particular situation, hoping rather than trusting that their intercession will carry more influence with the Divine Creative Force than our own requests ever would.

Our life experiences have taught that we cannot always trust our logical judgment, that situations can occur or unfold in a way that rational thought could not foresee or predict. Such instances can cause us distress, and cause us to fear the unknown. What we often don't realize is that sometimes our soul chooses these situations so that it might experience the full gamut of emotional states and through that learn to use hidden talents and abilities to achieve greater awareness; or sometimes a greater universal plan is unfolding that we are part of but are unaware of our role in its execution. This is why it is best not to enter into judgment as we are not seeing the whole picture. We have all heard stories of various individuals who upon getting a feeling, hearing a voice or just knowing not to go to a certain place or use a certain means of transport, trusted their intuition and avoided certain death or being involved in a particular drama.

Life on the physical plane has turned trust from a gift of integration and oneness to one of separation. Over successive generations humankind has been encouraged to be distrustful on many levels. We have been taught to distrust firstly ourselves, our own divinity and our inherent ability to create into physical manifestation our heart's desires. We have also been taught to distrust others, seeing them as potential enemies, and been given the message that we can only survive in this world if we distrust others. 'Trust no one but yourself' is a very sad indictment of where humanity has reached. This has been a constant theme throughout the history of humankind, and many wars and battles have been waged through one particular group or country distrusting another. It has on occasion brought civilization and humankind to the brink of annihilation as occurred during the Cuban Missile crisis in 1962 when Russia and America were on the verge of launching nuclear missiles which would have destroyed the world. It was averted only by an intuitive 'knowing' and trust – ultimately driven by the desire for the common good.

When we lose trust whether by our own actions, experiences or beliefs we cut off the lifeline that we have with the Divine Creative Force. We close down an awareness of our own divinity and instead set about building a fortress of fear around us that keeps us separate from our fellow humankind. Trust needs to be shared to be fully enjoyed and appreciated. If we trusted ourselves fully then we would never need to distrust others, as we would be confident in our own abilities to handle whatever situation we meet. Trusting ourselves means to be wholly and fully in contact with our Intuition using our Discernment as our guide in all situations. As Intuition comes from the higher self or soul which in turn is one with the Divine in fully trusting ourselves we really trust not only ourselves but also the Divine Creative Force.

It is the ability to trust with faith even when we cannot see the outcome or fully understand what is happening that allows us to grow spiritually. If we believe that right action is always taking place in our life and trust that we are being guided, life becomes easier to deal with and less fraught with fear and anxiety. Fear and anxiety stem from distrust in the process of life, not trusting that we are safe, being cared for and protected. We all have a survival instinct which we rely on and this instinct which is a tool of the mind predetermines the amount of trust that we will apportion to any situation or individual.

Trust based solely in judgment is limited as it relies on past experience and information gleaned from the five senses to make decisions. However, when used with intuition and discernment, trust becomes a divine gift which can transform not only the way in which we view life but also the choices we make. It opens and maintains the connection with the Divine Creative Force allowing us access to all the information contained therein, offering guidance and clarity in life. This permits us to walk fearlessly through the world confident in our ability to deal with all situations in a manner that befits not only ourselves but all of humankind.

Consider the following to help develop Intuition, Discernment and Trust...

- What is my intuition telling me in this situation?
- Does this feel right for me?
- If I choose this how will it be of benefit to me?
- What am I sensing from this person/place/situation?

Part 10

Forgiveness

Forgiveness is an act of Divinity that evolves from the practice of intuition, discernment and trust, and flows from the heart. When initiated from this position, it occurs effortlessly, surpasses logical thought and requires no exertion or drama. It is a level of consciousness that operates from a different vibrational level than any of the emotions that are the antithesis of forgiveness such as anger, hurt, revenge, disappointment, shame, guilt or hatred.

Inherent in the act of forgiveness is allowance. This may involve 'the allowance' that a situation has occurred which cannot be reversed, an act perpetrated that cannot be undone, a blow dealt that has irrevocably changed the course of the lives of those involved, words spoken that cannot be taken back, a chain of events unleashed that must run their course. In allowing the situation the individual is not plunged into the role of victimhood and helplessness. At this level allowance denotes surrender to a higher power, a conscious awareness that a greater purpose is being served; there is no judgment or repressed emotions just an inner awareness that it is as it is and that despite outward appearances divine order is being unfolded. When practiced, forgiveness allows healing to begin; it releases the person or people from the drama and emotions of that particular event, permitting them to move forward by defusing the emotional charge of that event so that when it is recalled it is not relived.

Forgiveness is total, it is not entered into on a partial basis nor is it based on conditions; it is either present or not. It emanates from the heart not the head, and is a flow of energy from the Divine Creative Force through the heart outwards towards the situation or person that is being forgiven. That energy transforms all that it comes in contact with, from the person through whom it flows to the events and all involved in them. It allows a new perspective to develop, one that is not caught up in the minutiae and the prevailing emotions of the event or the rightness or wrongness of things; both of which rely on judgment, but on a higher consciousness that can view the situation with compassion.

There is an awareness that within this episode there are souls who, by virtue of their beliefs and the experiences that they have had while on this Earth plane and indeed over many lifetimes, have taken decisions and carried out actions that were either not in their own best interests nor of those directly affected by them. This does not mean that they are to be exonerated from the effects of their words or actions, but there is an understanding that their level of conscious awareness has led them to this place. We cannot be totally sure that given the exact same circumstances, holding the exact same beliefs and having had the exact same life experience and level of awareness that we'd have done anything different. We'd like to think that we would and we certainly would have the choice, but we may not have chosen any differently. The old Native American saying, 'Do not judge a man until you have walked a mile in his moccasins' expresses the same sentiment.

When we are operating from the level of consciousness where forgiveness is an integral part of how we operate in the world, we make less definitive judgments about the 'rightness' and 'wrongness' of situations, and have an insight that we might not be getting the whole picture; there may be a greater performance being staged than our limited perception can comprehend. We also recognize that holding on to hurts, betrayals, injustices and loss is not to our benefit and only holds us in further suffering.

As our thoughts and beliefs create our reality, all the beliefs and emotions associated with an unwillingness to forgive will be operating in our lives. Each emotion calibrates at a specific vibrational level. Emotions such as shame, guilt, apathy, grief, fear and anger create a life that is centered in the past. It hangs on to the past reliving the emotion and drama of that time, creating misery and attracting into lives more situations at the same level of consciousness. A life lived in lower consciousness full of the emotions that are resistant to the joy of living is a much more challenging life as it is filled with emotions that numb, create discordance and erode peace of mind. And a lack of forgiveness can trap everyone involved in such a life.

When we choose to forgive we are taking a conscious decision to release each person from the energetic web that has held all stuck. We can use intuition and discernment to deal with the changes, challenges and decisions that initiating forgiveness may trigger, and trust the outcome of that process will bring freedom to all. This will be for many an uncomfortable experience, and may challenge the beliefs that are held around the righteousness of revenge and 'an eye for an eye'. We may not be able to conceive that it is possible or indeed right to forgive what we have judged as 'evil'. It will even be argued that in practicing forgiveness we are setting a bad example. We are giving others a ticket to behave badly, to not accept the consequence of their actions and to allow them to ignore the laws of the land, indirectly giving permission to terrorize and hurt the innocent and vulnerable. After all 'it only takes a few good men to do nothing for evil to flourish'. Forgiveness is even regarded in some quarters as a sign of moral weakness and an encouragement to evildoers or perpetrators to carry on without fear of retribution.

These concepts and beliefs were very much in evidence in some quarters after the atrocity that was 9/11 in the United States of America, when hijackers flew two airplanes into the landmark Twin Towers in New York, with the subsequent devastation and loss of life that followed. In the immediate aftermath of that attack following the shock, grief and anger there was a palpable desire for what many described as justice, a need to make someone pay. That heartfelt hurt, sorrow and sense of violation needed an outlet and focus. The intensity and rawness of the emotions being experienced demanded a response; someone or something was to blame, there had to be a reason, a cause, an explanation for the brutality and callousness that took so many innocent lives in this latest crime against humanity.

The outpouring of shock and grief on a worldwide basis signaled that a hitherto unseen line had been crossed. There was widespread fear and panic, both at individual and governmental level. People wanted reassurance, they wanted to feel safe again, more importantly they wanted someone to be held responsible for what had happened. The government wanted to be seen as in control and to send a message that it was not weak in the face of direct attacks on its citizens. The response which followed had its basis in that fear and panic, and embarked America (and with some other nations in tow) on a ten year war which has cost billions of dollars, the lives of thousands of people on both sides of the conflict and as yet shows no sign of resolution.

Yet as in all conflicts there is a point when those involved realize that there is nothing more to be gained by continuing in the manner that they have been doing, and that there has to a way to stop the killing and the discordance that has caused such agony for everyone and has cost so many lives. At some point in all conflict there is one person or group of people who are willing seek another way and to forgive in the knowledge that such an act is for the greater good. It is an act of bravery and selflessness for it involves setting aside or moving through their personal grief and trauma. There then begins the process of negotiating settlements and treaties which can require an inordinate amount of time to agree on. This is due in part to the huge emotional agenda involved and the fact that many on both sides are unwilling to forgive. The Middle East peace talks have been ongoing since the mid 1970s and as yet are not resolved. The Northern Ireland peace talks took a decade before agreement was reached.

An inability to forgive is not a modern-day phenomenon for humankind. History is full of accounts in which a perceived injustice or a difference in beliefs between leaders have plunged countries into war for decades, devastating lives, lands and the future of all involved in the upheaval. Mindsets have become hardened, beliefs more fervent and all involved are locked into a cycle of attack, reprisal followed by further attack. Similarly family feuds have travelled down over generations causing untold damage and hardship to all family members. After a few generations only a few remember the origins of the feud that has cost so much, but it is now a family pattern on both sides so it is carried on.

The Hatfield-McCoy feud (1878–1891) was one such infamous example. It involved two prominent families from the West Virginia/Kentucky border in the USA. It lasted 13 years, cost the lives of eight family members and began over the disputed ownership of a hog. When it finally stopped it was not that each side forgave the other; rather, as what happens in so many disputes, both on an international level and at a local level, a 'truce' was brokered – or on an international level this tends to be a treaty.

This essentially allows the atrocities and killings to stop, and is an agreement around negotiated codes of behavior and rules; but it does not heal the hurts held in the hearts and minds of all those who have been involved, nor is there any forgiveness involved in the process. That very much is a personal journey for each individual affected which will take time. So although the war is officially over all the emotions that this event created are still in situ, which is why skirmishes can be reignited with what only seems the slightest provocation. It can take generations before the ill feelings, suspicion and hatred of the opposing sides are neutralized and forgiveness can begin.

A most recent example of this on an international level has been the Truth and Reconciliation hearings that occurred in South Africa where there was a recognition that it was not just enough to repeal the Apartheid Laws that had been in operation there since 1948. Everyone had undergone so much hurt and had been affected so deeply by what had happened, that there needed to be a process of forgiveness on both sides that would allow each to tell their story, release the emotions associated with it, ask for and receive forgiveness to allow healing to begin. These Truth and Reconciliation proceedings, or Conflict Resolution Processes as they are referred to in some countries, have been carried out in war zones all over the world from the refugee camps in Bosnia to Sierra Leone, in an attempt to allow forgiveness to begin and the mental and emotional wounds of war to heal.

Forgiveness is an integral part of daily living on the planet Earth. Every day we encounter situations where we have to make decisions as to whether to hold on to perceived hurt or forgive the person, the action and the words spoken. The episodes may range from the banal to those whose repercussions have changed the course of lives irrevocably. Our lives, loves and relationships are based on our willingness to both forgive and be forgiven. The relationships we have with our friends, families and partners are predicated on their actions towards us and our actions towards them, how we react when we become hurt, whether we can forgive them, or in turn whether we are forgiven for something we have done to hurt them.

It is always a balancing act to make up our minds if the act merits forgiveness or not. In some cases we decide that we cannot forgive so great has been the effect and hurt; at other times we decide that we value the relationship, friendship or partnership more and are prepared to forgive or at least overlook indiscretions. In most of these incidences we come to our conclusion through weighing up the pros and cons in a logical way that comes from the head and rarely from the heart. We decide if we can live with the changes or the upheaval that will result should we choose to make an issue of our pain and demand contrition. In many instances we settle for ignoring or burying the pain concluding that we wish to keep things as they are and not upset the balance, or that the issue is not worth fighting for. It is always our choice.

There is also another aspect of forgiveness that we have to deal with on a regular basis and that is forgiveness of the self, for something we either did or failed to do. This aspect of forgiveness will influence how we live the rest of our lives, the decisions we take, the relationships we form, and how we view ourselves in terms of the type of life we feel we deserve. If we decide that an act we have committed is unforgiveable we may spend the rest of our lives consciously or subconsciously punishing ourselves for that choice. We will choose paths which will reinforce the beliefs that we hold regarding ourselves, for example that we are 'no good', that we are unlovable, we are untrustworthy, we do not deserve to succeed etc. It does not matter what the belief is, we will make it our business to ensure it becomes a self-fulfilling prophecy.

Once again this inability to forgive stems from judgment, in this case self-judgment. We have been actively encouraged from a variety of sources to judge ourselves on a daily basis that we might highlight defects in character and personality, and eradicate them by whatever means possible to achieve 'perfection'. Very few have provided a detailed definition of what this perfection might be; in fact if you were to ask a number of individuals what they would consider to be the 'perfection' as it relates to an individual, the responses would vary wildly and reflect the preferences of that individual as opposed to any definitive formulae. All we are aware of is that perfection is 'that which we are not at present'.

It is all too easy to spend a life in self-judgment during which we learn to despise what we perceive to be our weaknesses and mistakes while failing to recognize and appreciate that these events where we have 'failed' have been in fact an opportunity from the Divine Creative Force to experience something that we have on a soul level wished to experience, and have emerged from such situations a wiser, stronger person. The question that we need to ask on such occasions is 'What do I need to learn/know from this experience?' rather than 'How could I have let that happen?' When we ask the former question we are no longer in judgment, but rather in a place of expanding awareness; and it is this energy that allows us to have compassion for ourselves and to forgive ourselves for what we might regard as a moment of weakness. Self-forgiveness also allows us to be more compassionate towards others as we have an insight into the intricacies of decision-making and indeed how relying solely on our emotional state at the time as a barometer for our actions can lead to poor choices.

True 'forgiveness' is something that we rarely practice, and no longer value. While it is a word that is in our vocabulary we are unaware of its authentic meaning and potency. It is defined in the dictionary as:

A process of concluding resentment, indignation, or anger as a result of a perceived offence, difference or mistake, or ceasing to demand punishment or restitution.

In this context we can see how many situations that have caused great emotional upheaval and upset remain dormant within us not forgiven, waiting to be reignited or triggered by a similar occurrence at a later date.

Too often when we have had an altercation or disagreement we rush to resolve the unpleasantness and disharmony, sweeping the incident away by declaring that it is 'over' or that 'it doesn't matter'. We are not actually acknowledging the hurt and saying

'I forgive you'. We are merely stating that we don't really want to deal with the hurt that the actions have caused, and prefer to move on and carry on as if nothing has happened.

That, however, isn't what happens; and inevitably the accusations arise at some later point, usually when tempers are frayed, and the hurt reappears to be dealt with again. The counterarguments that 'you always bring that up' or 'you can't forget' will also resurface. The reason why this occurs is that the act of forgiveness was never initiated, and the energy and the memory of that hurt are as sharp and as poignant as when the incident occurred. When we truly forgive there are no recriminations, there is no alluding to past incidents; there is only forgiveness, the slate truly is wiped clean.

Forgiveness is a sacred act, one in which the person who has wronged another is truly aware of the impact that their actions or words have had on another, and requests the person they have wronged to release them from their wrongdoing by opening their heart and allowing the love to flow between them once more. It is essentially an act of 'heart'. It can only occur when those involved are totally honest and open in acknowledging what has happened, the hurt that the action or word has caused and a true regret on the part of the perpetrator matched with a true desire to repair the situation; or if that is not possible then to accept the consequences of their actions.

On the part of the person who has been wronged there must be a willingness to acknowledge that they have been hurt and that regardless of that hurt they are ready to open their hearts and allow that other person to connect with them again at the same level of intimacy that they previously enjoyed. In doing this they are also entering into an unspoken contract that they will not keep reminding the other of the incident, or use it to become a 'victim'.

In those incidents where the person who has caused the hurt is not personally known, the individual affected by their actions and who is now ready to forgive has to open their heart to forgive that person. This could be a parent who has lost their son or daughter through the actions of another, be it a drunk driver, a drug-fuelled act of violence, a murder or sniper's bullet. It does not matter how the act of forgiveness is an equally demanding step, requiring courage and a level of consciousness that steps outside the emotional turmoil surrounding the aftermath of the action to a higher consciousness, where all is acknowledged and yet the heart still opens. The energy required to complete this act is divine in nature, originating outside of ourselves yet fully integrating into our being once we have the intention to forgive. As it becomes activated there is the awareness that all are ready to move into the next stage of healing, to pick up the reins of a life that has been irrevocably altered and create something new that does not dwell in the past, but stays in the present taking one step at a time and living in the now.

So often this does not happen and true forgiveness never really occurs. There may be a tacit agreement by all involved to move on as no one wants to take responsibility for the consequences of their words or actions as they believe there was justification for their behavior. They will convince themselves that there were faults on both sides; and in the interest of preserving the relationship that they have it is better to 'start afresh', 'agree to disagree', 'say no more about the matter'. A desire to move from the uncomfortable situation they find themselves in to one in which they are more comfortable, to bury what has happened. Often the situation has reawakened feelings of buried hurt or feelings of shame that they do not wish to either experience or own. They urge the others to move on, to forget it, to begin again. For their part those wronged do not want to lose the relationship or to be seen as becoming a victim of the hurt. They also have had old hurts reactivated by the incident or words, and do not wish to be reminded of a time when they felt less than whole. They often agree without either acknowledging or moving through the hurt. On a logical level everything may have been worked out, reasons given and accepted, mediation may have occurred to allow a solution acceptable to both to be reached. However, these 'resolved' situations rarely last as the most important ingredient necessary for a peaceful and lasting outcome has been omitted and that is forgiveness.

This is readily seen in partnerships where one half has an affair. The emotional maelstrom created within the relationship is palpable as each partner tries to manage intense, diverse emotions. For the 'injured' partner there is the shock and disbelief followed by rage, betrayal, hurt, a recognition that the relationship is over, the trust broken and the fear of having to create a new life or relationship. For the other there are the emotions and feelings of shame, guilt, unworthiness, despair, a sense of loss and fear to be dealt with.

There may be after a period of time, when the emotional storm has settled, attempts at reconciliation where the couple try to either recreate the relationship they have had or develop a new one. This can occur following mediation or counseling when both parties sit down with an objective and trained mediator to rationally work out what went wrong, why it happened and where to go next. An agreement may be reached to either break up or to try again with a program implemented to start again. There will be remorse, the begging for 'forgiveness', the justifications for their actions and eventually an agreement reached on how to proceed forward; but unless this whole process involves forgiveness at a heart level then both parties are merely papering over the cracks of what is a flawed and unfulfilling relationship for both.

In situations where there is deep hurt, an emotional blockage is formed in a person's energy field. Other emotions build up and the flow of energy between themselves and the other individual is interrupted, anger, resentment, bitterness, and distrust develop and these emotions can explode out in an uncontrolled torrent on the next occasion they fear that they are going to be hurt again. This hurt can be so great that it affects every other relationship in their lives, coloring how they view the world and their place in that world. They can become stuck, a victim to their hurt, paralyzed by the emotional pain which becomes their personal mantra, unable to live the secure and happy lives they deserve. Over a period of time this emotional blockage and pain can manifest in the physical body causing havoc with personal health.

Many people acknowledge that they want to forgive but feel they can't. There can be many reasons for this, not least of which is that part of them that feels justified in holding on to the hurt, and conclude that in forgiving the offender they are somehow not 'honoring' their hurt. There is also the desire to remind the other person of their past actions and what they have created and the only way that they feel they can do that is by holding on to that hurt. In life what we focus on grows and our point of view creates our reality; so in holding on to the perceived hurt, our life is held in stasis and in some cases draws to us more of the same. We cannot move forward because the amount of energy necessary to maintain this point of view is immense and allows us little time or energy to create a life that would make us happy.

So how can this cycle be broken? The first step is deciding that it is time to forgive and let go, and in making the intention to forgive a gateway to the power of the Divine Creative Force is opened that allows a heart connection to develop. By asking the Divine Creative Force how to forgive this act or this person, you are then allowing the Divine Creative Force to provide you with a step-by-step action plan to accomplish this. It is revealed gradually and all that is required is a willingness to take the next step using intuition, discernment and trust as your guides. In each situation the action to be taken will be different and it will be personal to each person and their situation, taking into account their individual beliefs and preferences.

It will be revealed in a way that may appear coincidental, synchronistic or even magical, and all it requires is an awareness that an answer is being presented. For one individual the action intuited may be to go for a walk in nature and while doing that a heart connection may be established that gives them the courage to make a phone call and reestablish a relationship that had ceased because of unforgiven hurt; for another it may be to go into town where they might 'bump into' the person that they need to instigate forgiveness with. There is no one size fits all; each will be tailored to meet the needs of those involved.

When we begin the act of forgiveness the journey's end remains invisible to us. We know on a cerebral level that we no longer wish to harbor the emotions of lower consciousness that come with refusal to forgive, but often we are seldom prepared for the internal emotional spring cleaning that heart forgiveness can create, not just for us but for those receiving forgiving energy. It can be challenging, frightening, life changing, exhilarating and liberating. We face our fears, move through our pain, challenge our beliefs and remove our limitations. In participating in this act we are growing, not only as a person, but also on a soul level.

There are two aspects to forgiveness, initiating and receiving; this applies whether it is forgiving yourself or other people. We have discussed already the path to initiating forgiveness but there also an energetic process involved in receiving forgiveness. In this process the heart must open to receive the energy of forgiveness; in other words we must allow ourselves to be forgiven. The world today is full of people who cannot accept the forgiveness of others and so cut themselves off from receiving the purest love inherent in any act of forgiveness. They actually believe themselves to be beyond forgiveness or resentful of taking responsibility in the first place for their actions, seeing their behavior as being justified on some level.

They are the walking wounded, often they have become their

own judge and jury; and while a prisoner may look forward to release some day, these people walk the Earth locked in their own personal prisons of resentfulness, anger, self-loathing and fear. They cannot accept forgiveness, blocking the energy; and while it may emanate from the other person they refuse to be freed even though their cell door has been opened and all they need to do is walk through to enjoy the freedom from guilt that is being offered to them.

For those people resentful of the fact that they need forgiving or feel they have done nothing wrong, it is ego that prevents them from acknowledging their wrong; and even with those who feel they are too awful to be forgiven it is also ego that tells them it is so. In both cases the only person to suffer is themselves for they carry with them the energy blockage that is preventing love from flowing freely into their hearts; and in this planet of free will they have the right to make the decision to accept forgiveness or not.

So many people in the world believe that they have forgiven an act, a person, a situation because they logically in their mind have done so. They may even have uttered the words but if they have not opened their heart, if they have not released their hurt to the Divine Creative Force after acknowledging, feeling it and allowing the love of the Divine Creative Force to flow into that space, their words of forgiveness have no power; they are merely tools of the mind engaged in an intellectual exercise. Likewise it is often assumed by saying, 'I'm sorry' we are expressing contrition and requesting forgiveness; however, this in not always the case. For some it is uttered with no thought other than it is a series of words that absolves the speaker from any further responsibility for what has happened. It is used with such regularity, in such a variety of circumstances with such an array of meanings, that it now has little value other than as an expected polite phrase.

To truly forgive we need to use our words with meaning.

When we compare the potency of the words 'I forgive you' with 'Oh never mind, it doesn't matter' or 'Please forgive me' with 'I'm sorry' we can see that the intent in each of the two examples varies wildly. The use of the word 'forgive' elevates the request from a polite art form to a most sacred act, activating an energy that is greater than ourselves to reestablish 'heart connection' and prevent separation. Once completed with authenticity and integrity the process does not need to be repeated; it is finished and all involved are free.

Forgiveness is yet another powerful tool that we have been gifted with on our journey through life. In using it we are able to avoid falling into the role of victim or becoming trapped in a mindset that prevents us from being who we truly are or living the life that we truly wish to create. It does not mean that we will never experience hurt or that we will not meet circumstances and challenges that will change the expected course of our life. It does offer assistance and a grace to go through those events in a way that allows us to emerge victorious, a stronger, wiser and more compassionate person. In doing so we reflect our own divinity and release the power that lies within. Consider the following questions to initiate forgiveness...

- What do I need to learn/know from this experience?
- What do I need to do in this situation to begin the forgiveness process?
- What steps do I need to take to forgive this person?
- Where do we go from here so that forgiveness can operate in this situation?
- What steps do I now take to forgive myself for...?

Part 11

Emotional Investment

Human beings are creatures of emotion. It is how we experience the world in which we live and interpret the situations and events we encounter. It is the true currency of the Earth which we inhabit and is how we ourselves judge the quality of the interactions that we have and the people that we meet, by how they make us 'feel'. We are able to 'feel' a wide range of emotions across a wide and varied continuum, from those emotions which make us feel 'good' to those emotions that do not make us feel good.

Over the millennia each culture has developed an extensive vocabulary to try and capture each emotion, that we might share with one another the emotional state currently being experienced at any given time. Those emotions that make us feel 'good' we deem to be positive, and describe using a variety of words, including joy, gratitude, compassion, peace, happiness, serenity, forgiveness, love and so forth; those that don't make us feel good we regard as being negative and will use words such as fear, hatred, jealousy, anger, hostility, shame etc. to describe how we are feeling.

It has been argued that regardless of how many words we have generated to describe these emotional states there are basically only two at the core. The first is 'love' which is the main ingredient at the center of all those emotional states that make us feel good and in those states where we are experiencing our own true divine nature, at one with all in the Universe. Love is 'what we are' and 'to be the love that we are' consciously aware of our own divinity in all its magnificent glory is our mission on the Earth plane at this time. If we lived our lives from this premise we would indeed have heaven on Earth and inhabit the Utopia that deep within us we know can exist. We would look at each other with 'love' as opposed to the judgment that we currently use to separate ourselves from others.

The second group of emotions which we experience often leaves us feeling less than whole and has at its source an absence of love which is essentially fear. Fear creates within us separation, a belief that we are less than whole, isolated, alone and vulnerable. In this space it is very easy to visualize and create possibilities that feed on those lower vibrational emotional states. We have been given so much misinformation as to events occurring in the world and our own capacities and capabilities to cope with these situations, that as a result we have become trapped in the illusions and delusions of the 'ego' and its physical manifestations. We have become confused and have allowed fear to enter our lives as a reality within which we operate. This has meant that we are no longer aware of what or who we are; the simple truth that we are love incarnate has become lost as we seek to find meaning in our life by looking outside of ourselves to other people or things to provide it.

We are not born fearful. We learn to be fearful because we are told that this is the appropriate emotion to feel in a particular situation by those around us; initially it is our parents then it is our peers, teachers, media, and society, and once we learn the concept of fear then it is only a matter of time before we learn a new vocabulary to explain the discomfort that we are experiencing in situations when we are not being true to ourselves or have moved outside our comfort zone.

It is said life is simple but that it is man who complicates things. This would indeed appear to be the case, as over the centuries there are those who have sought to establish their own power structures and power bases by distorting this idea that love is our natural state by encouraging and even demanding that we see ourselves as unworthy and at the mercy of a vengeful God figure who has demanded 'an eye for an eye' and wants revenge on all perceived transgressors or wrongdoings.

Many of the world religions, regardless of their origins – whether Judaism, Christianity, Islam, Hinduism – have at some point in their histories lauded the virtues of 'Holy War', be it the Crusades in the 12th century waged by European Christians against the Islamic world or the Muslim 'Jihad' which literally translated means to strive or struggle in the way of God and have been undertaken in defense of Islam or as a means of converting other non-Muslim countries or peoples. Or even the Milkhemet Mitzvah (commandment war) of the Jewish religion, which is obligatory for all Jews regardless of gender and is limited to the protection of the territory within the borders of the land of Israel.

The leaders have deemed such wars as being in the name of 'God' and therefore it is implied they have had divine approval; all have insisted that it is the duty of every individual in that particular religion to take part in such wars and that the killing, maiming and destruction wreaked in the process justifiable, as after all it is done in 'God's name' and in his defense (as if a divine being would require defending).

Too often many of these so-called religious or holy wars have had political or economic consequences such as the removal of a particular individual or dynasty, land acquisition, or the control of resources or trade routes. These Church-State alliances often meant the true reason for the conflict had its origins in controversy and manipulation. The People have been taught that they have lost the love of their 'God' and must win it back by obeying a series of rules and regulations. And even more importantly, it is implied that they are incapable of achieving this without the direct intervention and intercession of the 'chosen ones' in each religion or state.

Scriptures have been produced to back up their claims and in each translation something has been changed, either added or taken away, to such an extent that if the original 'authors' ever returned to Earth they would have a difficult time recognizing their own work. A prime example of this exists in the Christian religion at the First Council of Nicaea in 325 AD, where it is said the Emperor Constantine and the bishops of the day met to decide what writings would be regarded as 'divine' and what others were to be destroyed. They also declared that Jesus was part of God, the son aspect of the Holy Trinity, and that the rest of humanity are and must remain separate from the Source. It was also in one of these Councils that reincarnation was written out of the Christian bible, as it was felt it gave too much power to the people. Anyone who disagreed with these positions could expect to meet severe punishment, even possible death.

Our direct relationship with the Divine Creative Force has been manipulated and complicated to suit the needs, desires, and gratifications of particular individuals and institutions at various times; and as a result we have become very far removed from our original connection with the Divine, much less able to actually recognize ourselves as an integral part of it. Each group does not see the whole picture, rather their own limited version of it and they present this personal view of what they perceive to be 'the truth'.

Their error is not in presenting 'the truth' as they see it, but rather in insisting that theirs is the only view. This has been the basis of all historical and religious wars on the Earth plane. Religions have ceased to be about helping everyone to be the love that they are, but have encouraged the ideas that not only are we all separate from the Divine Creative Force but we are different and separate from each other. This mindset has helped develop fear within each one of us.

This fear is further fed with sermons and orations on retribution, anger, revenge, and continues to grow ever bigger until we begin to perceive ourselves as powerless victims at the mercy of a vengeful deity intent on destruction. We do not stride fearlessly through the world sure in the knowledge that we are loved and cherished, but rather tiptoe fearfully afraid of everyone and everything. In this state people are much easier to influence and control. Their power base becomes stronger and humanity becomes a herd of sheep failing to recognize that those who call are not the shepherd but a pack of wolves dressed in the shepherd's clothing.

In much the same way 'love of country' has been manipulated to induce many young individuals into war to 'protect the homeland'. It has been presented as a noble and honorable thing; the words honor, duty, heroism and service have long been associated with war, and to lay down one's life for country or religion has been regarded as a noble and virtuous act. The horror of killing mass numbers of people and the damage that being witness to such acts has on the individual is minimized or ignored, as indeed are many of the veterans who return from war suffering from Post-Traumatic Stress Disorder. This is a prime example of how the concept of love has become twisted in the minds of humankind, and 'love' as violence or as abuse has been accepted as the norm.

On an everyday basis we can see that love is often associated with 'pain and suffering' and 'unrequited love' – the romantic notion of love of which pain, suffering, rejection and vulnerability are accepted parts, and all add to the drama of what we have been taught is love. The idea of the happy ever after is sold as the ideal outcome of a loving relationship; what we are not told is the 'how'. How do we achieve this? Is it achievable here on Earth or is it, as has been alluded, something that only happens in fairy tales and not representative of real life?

The concept of love, as played out in today's society, is often more to do with control and an economic agreement rather than a communion between two individuals that comes from the heart and not the head. We have grown very far away from the idea that humanity and the Divine Creative Force are one, and just as the Divine Creative Force is love so too are we. We do not need any intermediaries to intercede or mediate with the Divine

Creative Force on our behalf; we are well able to do that ourselves by going within to that quiet, still place within the heart and connecting directly with the Divine within ourselves.

The only thing that prevents such an occurrence is that we no longer trust ourselves, or we believe that we 'the sinners', 'the despised ones', 'the infidels', 'the outcasts' could have this wonderful gift within ourselves or that we have the inherent ability to master such a gift for our own benefit. We fear we might 'mess up', and risk the wrath of 'God'. We have been taught that we are unworthy of communicating with the Divine Creative Force directly, that such an audience requires perfection, something that obviously requires years of practice, specific training, many tests and initiations to achieve. We are lead to believe that this is the prerogative of the few specially chosen ones, not the birthright of all. These are the falsehoods perpetuated to keep the sense of isolation and fear strong within us. In truth the only thing really preventing us achieving this direct relationship with the Divine Creative Force and recognizing that we are love incarnate is 'fear'.

Fear is one of our most primal instincts, to act as an early warning device, to ensure survival on the planet. However, over the millennia it has evolved so that it is a response not only to imminent danger, which evokes a flight or fight response, but a sophisticated emotion that is triggered by all sorts of situations. It responds not only to visible dangers but also to invisible stimuli and affects every aspect of our daily lives; every action we take, every thought we think is often colored by fear. We act in a certain way and live our lives in a particular manner because we fear the reaction of our family and friends; we have fearful thoughts as to what would happen if a certain situation changed. For many the future may be viewed with fear and trepidation, fearful of the uncertainty and change, unsure of their ability to cope with these new situations.

Fear is the antithesis of both love and joy. We cannot live a full and fulfilling life if we are fearful. It can be the glue that holds us rooted in the past or stuck in the present, unable to move forward. Often this fear is not of our own making. It can belong to our parents, families and wider communities. It is what prevents us from being who we truly are and can often block us from achieving our true potential. We also, over our lifetime, add to our own fear bank. Left completely unchecked and unhealed many of our experiences in life can reinforce those fears we already carry or can create new ones as our fear-based beliefs come home to roost.

Fear is energy and like every other energy it vibrates at a certain frequency and in this case it vibrates at a level of frequency that ties in with other emotions, such as resentment, jealousy, helplessness and despair. These emotions we often regard as negative because they do not make us feel good about ourselves, and prevent us from being the love that we truly are. They hold us in a space where we become unsure of our own abilities, lose faith and trust in ourselves and the Divine Creative Force; very soon we have created a life that we are not happy with or one that causes us pain and distress, where our needs are not being met and we are experiencing lack.

It can be very difficult in this dark and lonely space to see a way out; we often seem to move from one crisis to another without any respite and this we accept as our life. This, we assume, is the life we were meant to have and is, we assume again, how we will continue for the rest of our time on this Earth. It does not, however, need to be so. But we become afraid of changing things, fearful that by 'rocking the boat' things may become worse. We console ourselves with the fact that at least we are in a situation in which we can 'cope'. We may be sitting on thorns but if we don't move we can endure the pain. Needless to say there is a way of reducing the fear that operates in our life and creating the life that we were meant to have; one in which our needs are effortlessly met. We do this by replacing one fearful thought with another less fearful thought.

This begins with the process of merely asking a question 'What if?' This opens us up to possibility and in the process we reduce our levels of fear. By continually replacing each fearful thought with another question and then another we eventually get to the space where our thoughts around that situation or individual are no longer fearful, and that allows us to find solutions to the original fear. In this way can we take charge of our lives and create a life that is fear free. We become more confident in our abilities to cope with whatever life throws our way and begin to trust ourselves more. Now that is not to say we never will encounter situations in which fear may be our initial emotion, but by asking questions 'How can I change this?' and 'What do I need to do now?' we are actually inviting the Divine Creative Force to help, allowing intuition and inner knowing to give us a series of solutions that will enable us to move forward and not stay rooted to the spot, isolated, alone and feeling helpless.

We have at our disposal the tools we need to first of all identify what we think the problem is and then to solve it. We are no longer bound by fear; we can move through it and as we reduce the number of situations that cause us anxiety we eventually become fearless. It is this that allows us to walk through our time on this Earth with joy, excitement and antici-pation. Situations or people which previously we would have viewed as terrifying, filling us with fear and dread, are viewed more as challenges. It is this change of attitude that allows us to transcend them and use them to our advantage. We no longer have to avoid things, people, or situations; we are able to meet them face on and with that approach many problems simply slip away or are solved more easily.

Fear can be controlled and managed to the extent it no longer becomes a major driving force in our lives but returns to its place of original purpose, as a springboard from which our greatest growth can occur. It can be the catalyst through which we see our own magnificence, and see what we are actually capable of achieving and creating; all we have to do is to be willing to move through it and claim our own divinity. As with anything we fear, the more energy we give it by consistently dwelling on it the bigger it becomes. This increases the power it has over us, allowing it to erect insurmountable limitations in our own mind to the point we become paralyzed, unable to see any solution. We all have different ways of coping with what we fear: for some it is worrying incessantly but never doing anything; for others, it is busying themselves with other things, ignoring it and hoping it will go away and that they won't have to face it; for another group they charge it head on and try to force their will so it becomes a battle to the death in which there can be only one victor.

So what do we fear? We essentially fear the judgment of others and their reaction to us based on their judgment. We fear rejection, punishment, isolation, being discovered as unworthy, not good enough, and a host of other imagined imperfections and negative reactions. When we begin to think of all the fears we hold, we become overwhelmed and mistakenly believe that in order to become fearless we must remove each individual fear and so prepare ourselves for a lifetime of work. However, the solution is much simpler; we do not need to go through the fears one by one, but straight to the source of the fear so that we treat the cause not the many and varied symptoms.

The thought that is at the foundation of all our fears is that we are alone, separate from the Divine Creative Force and have been abandoned here on this Earth to make of things the best we can. We do not even feel at one with the other humans and species that inhabit the Earth at this time. This feeling of separation, abandonment and aloneness has allowed fear to flourish in our life blocking the flow of love between ourselves and the Divine Creative Force. As a result we have decided we must protect ourselves and to hide our true nature. We do this by rationing our love, giving it to only those we deem special, those who meet our own individual criteria or are what we consider loveable. It has also caused us to doubt our own lovability, and many have deemed themselves unlovable or unworthy of love thus furthering the idea of separation in their lives. If we can subscribe to the notion that we are from the Divine and in that divinity there is nothing or no one that is greater than we are, then we will recognize fear for the illusion that it truly is.

We are then free to let love rule... without rules. Love as it is practiced here on Earth is conditional. It brings with it an element of exchange and has its roots in judgment. For example, 'I will love you if you do this...' 'It is because I love you that I am telling you...' It is often used in a very destructive and abusive manner to control, manipulate or disempower another; this is not love in the divine sense of the word. Love as an energy holds no conditions; it comes from the heart and has no need or desire to control or manipulate. There is only the desire for communion with another and an awareness of that individual as a divine being who like you has been given the gift of free will to make the decisions that are best suited to them. In allowing them to make their decisions without judgment you too have free will to decide if you will follow them on the path they have chosen, or choose something that is right for you. There is no drama, blackmail or emotional meltdown; it is in this environment that true cooperation can occur and agreement reached.

We all have an inner knowing that we are at our best when we are in a loving state for then we can freely embody all the qualities of love, compassion, kindness, caring, gentleness, giving and receiving that we truly are. However, so many of us feel that these states are not compatible with our daily lives and that indeed if we were to be 'love' all of the time that we would be judged as weak or deluded, and would be taken advantage of by others.

We have been taught that 'to be the love that we are' is neither the rule nor practical; in fact it is seen as abnormal. Let's face it, if someone came into our life embodying all the qualities of unconditional love could we accept them? Or would we send them away convinced that they were a fraud or trying to dupe us in some way. We have been taught at an unconscious level to fear love and more particularly unconditional love; the underlying belief being that it will interfere with our ability to conquer life and compromise our ability to survive. As a result of these erroneous beliefs we are also reticent to receive love, and feel we must somehow limit the love we allow ourselves to receive and the number of people from whom we will accept love from.

In order to do this we must judge others either as being worthy or not; unfortunately this brand of 'love' has its limitation as it comes from the head and not the heart. It relies on our judgment of others which is always at best flawed. How many times have those we deemed worthy of our love let us down, failed to live up to the expectations we had of them or failed to give us what we consider love? Often we discover that this 'love' is not as fulfilling as we first thought; we have not achieved the satisfaction or the fulfillment that we thought it would. We still feel empty, something is missing; we can't find it or don't know exactly what it is but we do know it is not present in the situation we are experiencing.

So what do we do? For some that is the point at which they begin looking for someone or something else, so sure are they it is out there but that they just haven't found it yet. For others they may decide that they will accept what is on offer and make the best of it, or they may decide that Love is an unobtainable idea and we on this Earth plane are not meant to experience true love and can only experience it when we die and move to another level or dimension be that Heaven or Nirvana. And yet love is so very obtainable by each and every one of us on a daily basis within our own lives. To achieve this love we need to become aware that what we seek is not to be found outside ourselves but within. One of the first steps in achieving this is to stop judging ourselves. We spend so much of our time analyzing what we did, what we said, how we look, what we should have done and what we should have said, how we think we should look that rarely do we actually give ourselves credit or appreciation for who we are or what we have achieved.

Once again we have accepted the notion that we can only do better if we find every fault and rectify it; so it would seem that we are always on a crusade to flush out every perceived imperfection. We are often our own worst enemies and harshest critics; for many, a large proportion of the self-talk engaged in is abusive, offensive and defamatory, creating feelings of unworthiness and being unlovable. It is small wonder given this behavior that we have little love or respect for ourselves and that we draw to us others who physically manifest what we ourselves are thinking.

We need to stop the harsh self-judgment and criticism; this may be going against the habits of a lifetime and indeed what we have been taught is appropriate behavior; but in doing this we open ourselves to developing self-approval and self-love. We cannot love another unless we first love ourselves. So in every situation that we find ourselves beginning the critical self-talk we merely say 'I am not going to judge myself on this'.

This does not mean that we never evaluate what has happened, but we leave out the destructive energy and words that tear at our very being and leave us feeling a failure. We use our intuition and discernment to decide what went well and what aspect of the situation we do not wish to experience again. In this way we learn and can move forward from a position of power as opposed to getting stuck in fear and self-loathing.

We can only reveal the love of the Divine Creative Force if we begin to recognize the love within and treat ourselves with the love, dedication and devotion that we so often reserve only for that 'special other'. When we do this we acknowledge our wholeness and completeness and are now in a position to improve all our relationships and create new relationships that are more enjoyable, loving and fulfilling. The quest for the perfect relationship or perfect partner is something that at some point is the primary focus in almost everyone's life. So often we enter relationships 'looking for something'. We say all we want is to be loved, to love and share love, but each of us have our own version of love and our own agenda; for each individual love means something different.

Love as it is used in today's society is merely a term used to convey very different needs. For some it may be the need to be wanted or it may be to remove the isolation and loneliness felt, or it may be the need to be part of something or to do what everyone else is doing. It may be the desire for children that sparks the search for a partner; whatever the cause, whatever the need, the bottom line is the same. It is essentially a search for a partner, for someone to fill the 'hole' that exists within us, the feeling that something is missing in our life. There are also the societal and cultural norms that demand that at a certain age you 'find love', marry, have children and continue the bloodline, ensuring the continuation of the species.

The search for love then takes on a new sense of urgency as the quest for a suitable partner is undertaken in order to fill what is for many their life purpose. They are quite willing to be swept off their feet, to get carried away in the game and fulfill their familial and societal obligations. The first flush of love ignites something within us. It awakens the sense of being connected, of being one with another; and the joy of that allows our heart to open and we find ourselves behaving in a way that we wouldn't normally. We become more thoughtful, more caring, we want to increase that other person's happiness and we try to think of ways that we could do that, regardless of the personal cost to us.

We are ruled by our heart not our head, and in this state we truly express who we are. Unfortunately this stage rarely lasts because along with many of our actions come expectations as to how that other person will think, feel and act. We expect them to return our thoughtfulness and kindness, behave in particular ways that we would like and when this doesn't happen we become disillusioned, upset or even angry. Their failure to 'read our minds' will cause us to react in a variety of ways: we stop making the effort or trying, either settling for the mundane or moving on. In some cases we develop a pattern of behavior that is of benefit to no one, and is more to do with routine than it is to do with love.

Another aspect in the search for love is our willingness to receive love from another; so many of us think that we are so unworthy of being loved that even when the perfect person, the perfect relationship shows up we are unable to welcome it. We can have a very set idea of how it will look, feel, be; and so when our expectations are not met, we begin to find fault, dismiss it out of hand deeming it too good to be true. The bottom line is that we believe we are not worthy of love or of being loved and as a result will reject what is on offer.

When we are not truly 'being', we may adopt a demeanor or set of views that we believe will please the other person in the relationship. We may pretend to like what they like, do what they do and essentially behave in a manner that reinforces similarities as opposed to differences. This we have been taught is the art of compromise, and is a necessary component in any relationship. There are, we are given to believe, many traits of character that are not conducive to good relationships and either must be hidden or repressed. In days gone by there were very strict codes of behavior which both genders were obliged to live by. In modern times and in most Westernized cultures these have been relaxed so that a more equal balance of power exists within the relationship. Nevertheless we still feel under pressure to hide aspects of character or behavior that we believe will not be accepted by the other person. We are essentially afraid that we will be judged by the other and deemed unworthy of their love.

Once, however, we become comfortable within the relationship as creatures of habit we soon resort back to our previous behavior, becoming less mindful and begin again to work on autopilot. The head begins to rule the heart and likewise our partner becomes equally tired. This can mark the end of what many call the 'honeymoon period' and the reason given is often that life demands prevent the continuation of such behaviors. It is at this point that many begin to question their choice. We have looked to another to fulfill our needs, to give us what we need in life not only on a physical or material level but also emotionally and spiritually. There is an unspoken desire for that other person to make us whole, and when that doesn't happen we become upset, disillusioned and angry. We feel we have been duped, made a bad choice or decide we must not have really been in love in the first place, which can result in many people becoming embittered and damaged by the experience.

Society has led us to believe that there is only one person out there for us and when we find them we will spend the rest of our lives living happily ever after. The divorce rate and breakup statistics are testament to the fact that this is not so. Many people are becoming more realistic, and realize that this is not always going to be the case; and the love and happiness they seek can often not be found by looking to another person to provide it but rather by looking within themselves, taking responsibility for their own happiness. Awakening the love within themselves, firstly for themselves and then for humanity; as the love within them grows it begins to spread out from them to include all humankind. They are whole, complete and can truly share their lives with another. They are no longer the needy individual looking to another to make them happy. When they are truly able to be the love that they are, then they have a choice to share that love with another or not. They are not diminished by either decision but are sure in their connectedness to humankind, seeing the divinity in others at peace within themselves and their role in life expressing themselves truly as the love that they are.

This is not a dream. It is within reach and obtainable by merely releasing the fear and allowing the love to flow in its place. In this ever-changing world in which we live, life itself has been moving faster and faster; things which we took as certainties and unchangeable truths are no more, they have been swept aside in the ever-growing torrent of change which seems to increase at an alarming rate each year. We can feel things are outside our control, and fear we may not be able to cope as our predictive abilities, which have been the basis of our survival, are no longer the true barometers they once were.

In such situations many are looking for something or someone to cling to, believing that in certainty comes stability; and while this holds good on some occasions it does not for every or all. It is often in times of greatest instability that if we are open we can learn the most; and here on the Earth at present we are going through a period of accelerated learning when life lessons are coming swiftly. Barely have we caught our breath after one drama then we are hurled into another; for some of us we seem to be permanently sitting on the horns of a dilemma of one sort or another. It can seem that we have little time to learn the lesson from one event before we face yet another lesson. This is part of what the soul came on Earth to experience and what we signed up to before we came to Earth.

The greatest mistake is to take it personally. The soul does not personalize things although it may feel like it. The soul wants the opportunity to experience and will seize every opportunity that comes its way to master challenges using its talents and abilities to experience the emotions held within that situation. If we understand this we can see that it is often not 'God' that is the cause of all our experiences but 'we are', or rather our soul is in its quest for further development to strengthen its connection with the Divine.

The presence of love in our life will ease that process; for many of us it will necessitate releasing limiting beliefs that we have about love and its place in our lives. The love that we speak about is a love without conditions that is divine in origin, infinite and abundant. It both gives and receives, and we need to be willing to receive love and not to have limits on how much we deserve and how that love will be presented. When we stop the self-judgment we allow ourselves to become more of our authentic selves and are free to express ourselves as the love we truly are. Consider the following...

- What in this situation is giving rise to the fear I feel?
- What question can I ask myself that will reduce my fear/anxiety/anger which I am experiencing?
- How can I help myself to resolve this feeling?
- What did I do really well in this situation?
- How can I show appreciation to myself today for being me?
- How can I change this?
- What if...?

Part 12

Abundance

Abundance is something that we as humans all aspire to and 'having abundance' is something that many work all their lives to achieve. It is for many the Holy Grail that they hope to reach, a point in life when they move past the worry and stress of survival and create a very different life to that which they have now. It is the position from which many believe that they will begin to 'live', a place where life becomes effortless, problems float away and happiness begins.

Abundance means different things to different people: for some it can be having a surplus of money with the ability to purchase anything they want when they want with no thought as to whether they can 'afford' it; for others it can represent the acquisition of rare and valuable objects; for some it represents freedom, being the masters of their own time with the liberty to choose; or for others it may be a sense of peace and security that comes with the knowledge that there are financial reserves to meet all emergencies; or it may simply be having a place to live with more than enough food to feed their families.

The actual details will vary depending on the individual's belief system and circumstances, but for the majority of humankind abundance refers exclusively to the procurement of material wealth. We consider ourselves to have abundance if we drive expensive cars, live in large houses, have a well-paid job, wear the latest designer clothes and buy the most up-to-date gizmos etc. It is not just about having 'enough' in the modern-day definition of abundance. There must be a surplus that is ever flowing, and must continue indefinitely with no break in supply or delay in delivery; only then do we consider ourselves to be abundant.

However, true Abundance involves so much more; it is first and foremost 'energy' with its own energy signature a specific vibrational frequency at which it oscillates. It is this energetic signature of abundance that we are all either consciously or unconsciously seeking. It is not merely confined to the acquisition of material wealth although that is part of it; but it is having an unlimited supply of everything needed to live a joyful, peaceful and meaningful life, and that includes an abundance in health, love, joy, happiness, peace of mind, life-affirming relationships, soul growth and conscious awareness from which true fulfillment comes. In fact for some spiritual devotees true abundance would be regarded as a state of inner peace from which nothing is desired or sought, but all can be created as needed.

As energy, abundance is neither positive nor negative. It is the meaning we give it that influences how it manifests into our lives. As we are all beginning to recognize, our thoughts create our future, and the emotions that we bestow on these thoughts coupled with the belief systems which operate in our lives create our experiences. So if we focus on and nurture thoughts and feed these thoughts with intense emotion and beliefs that accentuate the lack we perceive in our lives then it is this the Divine Creative Force will deliver an abundance of.

We create and draw to us the very things that we are trying to avoid through consistently thinking about and emotionally living our fears and perceived lack, whether that lack is of health, finances, meaningful relationships, or a lack of success in business. Our own self-talk is very powerful and is one of the more potent ways in which we can manifest and maintain these perceived lacks in our life. It is the saboteur that prevents us from creating the life that we desire, keeping us stuck in the vibrational frequency of fear and need rather than where we could be, in the vibrational frequency of abundance.

At present many people are identifying areas of their lives

that are not working. We are all undergoing a mini life review in which our errant beliefs and ideas are being highlighted to us in glorious 'Technicolor', and with an intensity hitherto unknown that we might become aware and change or eradicate them improving our lives in the process. This process involves not only identifying the limiting beliefs that have held us hostage during much of our lives, but there has to be a willingness to replace them with beliefs that have a much higher vibrational frequency, if we are to allow the energy of positive abundance to move into our lives. As always we have free will to decide what we wish to do but in order to make better choices we must first be aware of what is happening and recognize that the challenges which we are now being presented with we have faced before, just in a different scenario; and that held within those challenges is a belief or idea that is limiting us.

This is currently being demonstrated on a global level by the economic recession that appears to be engulfing most of the Western world. Initiated by a global banking crisis individual governments have now set about imprinting on their citizens the consciousness of scarcity and fear that there is not enough. The populace is being told that there 'will be pain', that they 'must take the pain' that it is their 'patriotic duty to endure the pain', and that this pain is indeed necessary and cannot be avoided, all of which brings to the fore many long-held beliefs and fears around the nature of abundance and the experience of lack.

If the truth be told there is no need for anyone to take 'the pain', least of all the majority of the population at whom it is directed and who are bearing the brunt of cuts in services and monetary losses. There are many who believe that this is a deliberate position to intimidate and create fear so that communities remain fearful, believing themselves powerless in the face of such crises. What if those in positions of authority had a belief system that included the concept of 'oneness' and recognized that we are all interconnected and that abundance is the birthright of all?

They would indeed use their power to create policies and protocols that would ensure enough for all by engaging with the Universal Laws of Abundance to create for the good of all. However, that is not what they have chosen, and instead have put their trust in 'the markets' and financial institutions which appear to function on rumor, innuendo and risk with the result they have created a society bound by fear, scarcity and need. This position has triggered in many individuals the dread that they may be forced into poverty, losing all they possess, and for some that indeed has become the reality that they find themselves in.

Others have chosen not to accept this viewpoint and are ignoring the limitations that are being imposed. They have set about using the challenges they find themselves in to turn their lives around and start afresh creating livelihoods and businesses that express more accurately who they are and which are closer to the lives that they came here on Earth to experience. These individuals are creating an abundance of wealth in their lives at a time when they are being told by the 'economic experts' that it is not possible. Warren Buffett an American business magnate, investor, and philanthropist is a point in fact, who has to date made 33 million dollars and counting in a market deemed volatile and in recession. What separates these individuals from the many in society is not some super human strength or insight; rather it is the belief systems that they hold.

If you were to ask both groups if they would like abundant wealth in their lives they would both say yes; but one group would tell you that that is not possible now as there is a recession while the other would ask the questions: 'How can I make that happen? How can I create a new business/more money/a well-paid job' and then tap into their own intuition, discernment and trust knowing that the response from the Divine Creative Force will come allowing them to be in the right place and right time to take the action to manifest their request into reality.

In asking a question they are immediately tapping into the wisdom that exists in the Divine Creative Force and have now initiated a process whereby they have put the Divine Creative Force on notice that they are stepping into their power as a co-creator and are ready to accept abundant wealth and the change that comes with it into their lives. The other group who have made the recession a part of their reality have made a statement and come to a conclusion, and in that statement they have handed away their power to create to others in perceived positions of power. As a result they have limited their options and the wealth they will accept or receive in their lives.

This very ably highlights the dilemma that we all encounter when dealing with the concept of abundant wealth, and that is while we all express a fervent desire to have abundance in whatever form is important to us, we may not be in a position to receive it into our lives. This can seem initially at odds with what would appear to be the common belief that everyone should have abundance and that as divine beings having an Earthly experience we should all have the same ability to create and actualize abundance within our lives.

While it is true that we all have the same potential, our abilities will vary considerably depending on our life experiences to date and the belief systems that we have inherited from our ancestral and cultural heritages with regard to accepting abundance. We may have a set level of abundance beyond which we either consciously or subconsciously reject what is being offered. We may not even be aware that we have such a principle; in fact these ideologies may not even be ours, but be among those that we have unconsciously accepted from our family, peers, religious or cultural society. There are few religious dogmas that extol the virtues of an abundance of wealth over poverty. In fact it is intimated that to have an abundant life is an unnatural state and one that we as humans should not expect on this Earth plane.

It is further implied that even 'God' himself is adverse to an abundance of wealth as the Christian bible declares, "It is easier for a rich man to go through the eye of a needle than to enter the kingdom of heaven." We also ascribe certain characteristics to those perceived to have an abundance of wealth; these include e.g. greed, arrogance, selfishness, self-centered, unfeeling etc. These judgments are applied without any discernment, and yet they could be as easily attributed to someone who finds themselves trapped in a cycle of poverty that leaves them fighting for their very survival. Small wonder that we might have within our belief system a rejection of wealth lest we be judged as harshly and treated accordingly. It is not enough to desire abundance; we must ensure that our belief system can support it.

Being open to 'receiving' is as an important aspect in the manifestation of abundance in whatever form as the asking; it is an equal part of the formulae 'ask and you shall receive'. It is in essence very simple: if we can't receive then how does abundance enter our lives? The Divine Creative Force always stands ready to present us with what we have asked for but often our own thoughts, beliefs, ideas and limitations prevent us from receiving that abundance. We will have all sorts of reasons and justifications as to why what we have requested has not actualized, from: 'This manifestation process doesn't work, it is a con' to 'It was too good to be true' or 'I always knew I wouldn't get what I asked for', 'I never get what I ask for', or even 'Life doesn't work like that, it is meant to be a battle, this would just be too easy'.

As we move into making judgments and drawing conclusions we automatically shut down our ability to receive the energy of abundance. We become victims as we seek to blame the process or forces outside ourselves without ever asking the questions: 'What is stopping me from having abundance in my life?' 'What beliefs and limitations do I have that are preventing me from being vibrationally compatible with the energy of abundance?'

In answering these we begin to unravel what is stopping us

from stepping into our power and gaining insight as to what we actually believe and how our lives and ultimately lifestyles are being controlled by those beliefs. In refusing to play the blame game we start to identify what might be getting in the way and move from the role of victim to being empowered as a co-creator in our own lives. It is then that we can decide do we wish to hold on to those beliefs or are we ready to let them go and replace them with those that will no longer limit.

For many the desire to be 'rich' in monetary terms is equated with abundance. Research carried out in this area indicated that when probed further and asked exactly what figure correlated with being rich, the figure varied wildly from individual to individual, reflecting the belief system that each has around wealth and money. It was reflective of what each would feel comfortable with having, rather than a specific monetary value. While many claim a desire to be rich, they are afraid of the change that such energy would cause in their lives and indeed the adaptations that they would have to undertake to integrate it into their lives.

In order to receive we sometimes have to let go of the familiar and let go what is no longer serving us; that may be a relationship, a job, a home, and that will challenge many. Suddenly people become aware that to accept abundance they will have to make changes, perhaps move house, neighborhood or that they might be treated differently by family or friends, or be seen by others as a meal ticket. They might have to cope with others asking for money or indeed be besieged by those hoping to gain from their good fortune and abundance. Then there is the fear of perhaps losing their money, having it taken off them either by force or through the unscrupulous behavior of others. All the fears and limitations around having money or wealth come to the fore and suddenly many who declared their desire to have unlimited wealth begin to set limits on what or how much they are willing to receive with the familiar holding more attraction than the unknown.

For many it is the fear of judgments by others for having money that they dread or at least are apprehensive about, for they realize that when good fortune appears to land on one person there are many who do not celebrate that gift, but rather become jealous and resentful of the other's apparent blessing. Monetary abundance can generate a lot of reaction from others and not all of it is positive because one person's acceptance of wealth can trigger the limited belief system in others. There are few who on hearing of another's 'luck' will genuinely feel pleased for the individual and exhibit that generosity of spirit that allows the energy of abundance to flow freely, demonstrating an inner knowing that abundance is a natural state that can be created by all and not by just the chosen few.

This generosity of Spirit cannot exist in an atmosphere of judgment, and it is an aspect of our being that is actively discouraged in a world where it seems that we have to justify our receiving. We have to both prove and be proved worthy of receiving, and when abundance appears in our lives then the scrutiny is intensified and the judgment increased. In today's society where scarcity has become the norm abundance in another's life is as likely to prompt the question: 'Why them and not me?' It is then that true beliefs can be voiced: 'I never win anything, I never get anything'. It is no wonder that while it may appear on the surface that we all crave abundance, in our lives it seems there is a caveat on how much we are willing to accept or deem ourselves worthy of accepting into our lives. It is in such situations that if we are aware we can catch our own self-talk which will truly reveal the attitude we have to abundance, not the one we think we have.

In Colombia, South America, so afraid are some people of being kidnapped for their winnings that many contestants on the *National Lottery Show* often appear in disguise or wearing masks over their faces in case they are recognized and they or a family member targeted by kidnappers. This again highlights that if there is not a positive correlation between our belief system and our desires, then we will not have the peace of mind that will allow us to accept abundance in our life with the ease, joy, grace and gratitude necessary firstly to attract it and then to maintain it.

We will essentially be incompatible with the vibrational frequency of abundance and are less likely to enjoy the abundance gifted to us by the Divine Creative Force. This may well explain why 80% of lottery winners will after two years have spent or lost their winnings, and will have returned to the same life that they had prior to their win. The win did not increase their level of happiness or relieve the stresses of life; many were unable to reconcile themselves with the changes that such an event caused in their lives. In effect they were unable to be at ease and peace with money, and so sought to get rid of it so that they could return to the familiar.

Another important aspect in the art of manifesting is that action is also required. Having abundance requires action; it is not enough to demand from the Divine Creative Force an abundant life and then sit about waiting on the Divine Creative Force to serve us. That may happen on some occasions but we chose to come on this Earth to experience life in a body moving around, encountering difficulties and challenges, but taking action in tune with the Divine Creative Force to move on and overcome them.

It is in these challenges that soul growth occurs and that we learn the extent of our capabilities and abilities as we overcome what appears at first insurmountable; it is through taking action that we become a co-creator rather than a passive observer in life. In this reality the general perception is that in order to 'have' we must 'do'. We must prove ourselves deserving of what it is we wish to have and the only way of achieving this is through struggle, effort and hardship. In fact it has come to be accepted that the greater the struggle and effort, the more justified and deserving we are.

While it is necessary in this world to take action, the type of action we take is important; it is not about 'doing', rather it is about 'being', and it is in the being that the action becomes effortless and flows. We become aware of what we need to do as we open a direct line to the Divine Creative Force and have an inner knowing of the next step to take. We do it without the struggle, effort and anxiety that would have previously characterized our action. In doing this we remove ourselves from the outcome sufficiently to allow it to enter in a way that serves our highest good and in a way that follows divine order.

It is often at this point that we can become disillusioned and upset, particularly if we have a set idea on the outcome and how it will appear we can undo all our good work at this point by fretting and engaging in self-talk that diminishes and countermands our initial request. If we can make our request from a place of curiosity and joy and in the form of a question without being attached to the outcomes then we are more likely to succeed in our quest to have our requests actualize into physical form. This may for example mean we ask the questions: 'Divine Creative Force or Universe, how can I create to have enough money to pay all my bills?' 'What do I need do to create more money to make that happen?' As opposed to 'I haven't got the money to pay my bills, I need more money and fast. Divine Creative Force, you have got to give me money now!' In questioning, the individual is open to possibility and the Divine Creative Force will begin to send answers to meet that request as opposed to the latter, which is a series of statements that focus on the judgment that there is not enough. Notice how different the energy is in both scenarios and the underlying emotion behind each.

It has been said that we can create more abundance from a position of joy than any other state, and that money follows joy not that joy follows money, as demonstrated by our lottery winners. Joyfulness is our natural state; when we feel pure and total joy we are at one with the Divine Creative Force and we are expressing ourselves and our vibratory being in the way that we were intended to be. This may seem incredible, as we appear to spend so little of our time in our day-to-day existence in that state that we consider it the exception as opposed to the rule. How has our natural state of joy come to feel more alien than all the negative feelings we experience?

We view it as something outside ourselves rather than something we have in abundance within us. We have come to expect that a good phenomenon has to occur in order for us to experience joy, and then the feeling will only last on a temporary basis; that something horrible will come along to burst our bubble. While true that a positive experience can add to our joy it does not need to be the catalyst for us to feel joy. The ability to be in a joyful state is merely a choice.

With children we can see how joy bubbles up within them, when often we as adults can see no apparent reason for their joyfulness. We assume it is because they have no worries or that everything is bright and new to them. We marvel at their ability to find joy in things which we take for granted; simple pleasures which for us hold no importance are reveled in by these new souls on Earth, and joy derived from them. It can be splashing in a muddy puddle, rolling in snow, or running through a pile of fallen leaves, or just making funny faces with a friend that can cause an outpouring of joy. In fact all these children are doing is living in the moment; they are not ruminating over the past or trying to predict the future. They are simply enjoying the moment. But very quickly that outpouring is stopped as children are taught that such joyous spontaneous eruptions are not allowed, they are frowned on by those around them, they are told they are being too loud, inappropriate, not in control of their emotions, and soon they learn to stifle this emotion in order to fit into what society demands.

So what is joy? Joy is a yet another energetic vibratory force that is the manifestation of love in action. It too has its own unique vibrational signature; this high-energy vibration has a positive effect on our physical, mental and emotional state. When we feel joy our heart soars, we feel everything is possible and we forget our self-imposed limitations; we feel at one with everything and experience a safety and security, a sense of belonging that we do not normally have. What if we could have that experience on an ongoing basis? How different would our outlook on life be?

What if we met all the challenges in life from a position of joy and possibility? Would Life feel like a struggle or would it morph into an experience where all was possible and all that it was dependent on were the choices we made? Would the energy of abundance be flowing or the energy of scarcity? This may once again feel unobtainable because we have been conditioned to believe that life has to be difficult to be 'meaningful' for us to 'learn', 'atone', 'gain enlightenment'. What if the only thing standing between us having an abundant life full of ease, peace, contentment and joy were the beliefs that we have and the limitations we put on ourselves as a direct result of those beliefs, which ultimately is reflected in the choices we make.

Would we be willing to step over the perceived limitations in every situation and ask: 'What else is possible?' allowing the Divine Creative Force to take over and present us with possibilities that we never even considered? Would we be open to having the abundance of wealth running through every area of our life without limitation or impediment? The choice as always is ours. In asking for abundance in our lives we are actively engaging with the Divine Creative Force and are requesting change; we are willing to have a new experience that may go against the beliefs which we were programmed with but one nevertheless that we are willing to embrace, and move through the feelings that such changes will engender. We are stating that we are ready to receive more in our lives and move into our power as co-creator that we might truly live as a divine being here on Earth with joy, peace and ease.

So how abundant are you? An interesting exercise to discover the belief system that you hold on abundance or money in your life is to write down the amount of money that you think you would accept if you were to be given it tomorrow. Then write how you would spend it and the changes or adjustments you would have to make to accommodate that amount in your life. Notice the feelings that this engenders and any self-talk that emerges as you complete the task. Who do these beliefs belong to? Are they yours or have you just absorbed them from the family or society you were brought up in. What limiting beliefs around abundance are no longer serving you?

We often have no idea of the beliefs that we hold around abundance. One way of capturing these beliefs is writing down the beliefs that your mother had around money, rich people, and a wealthy lifestyle; do the same with your father and both sets of grandparents. Write another list of beliefs you heard about abundance from the religion you or your parents were brought up in, the school you went to, the friends you had or indeed have. You will then have a blueprint of your financial beliefs and history. It is then that you can decide on which beliefs are serving you or not. Those that are no longer serving you rewrite on a separate piece of paper and either tear up or burn. This physical activity will send a strong message to the subconscious that you are releasing that thought form.

Then how do we know what action to take? In asking a question we are tapping into the wisdom of the Divine Creative Force. We can simply ask: 'Divine Creative Force what can I do that will help resolve this situation, or what action can I take that will actualize the money I request, the job I desire, the relationship that I am ready for?' Then listen. You may get an image, an idea, or a very clear sense to do something, go somewhere or even it may be to wait, just be aware.

Another way is last thing at night just before you go to sleep, hand all worries, anxieties and doubts to the Divine Creative Force/Universe with a request for guidance on what action to take. When we sleep we are in a state of neutrality and so more open to guidance from the Divine Creative Force. Upon waking in the morning notice what you are being shown or being told to do, be aware of the 'hunches' and 'intuitions' you receive. It may be something as simple as making a phone call, or meeting a friend for coffee. In taking these actions you are allowing the Divine Creative Energy to place you in the right place at the right time so that your request can be answered. Stay out of your own way by not rationalizing or overthinking things; in that way you allow your inner knowing to come through. Let's face it, if rational thought were the answer you would have had things figured out a long time ago. Consider the following questions...

- What is stopping me from having abundance in my life?
- What beliefs and limitations do I have that are preventing me from being vibrationally compatible with the energy of abundance?
- What is stopping me from receiving all the abundance I desire?
- What action can I take that would allow me to create even more abundance in my life?
- If I could have anything in my life right here right now, what would I choose?

Part 13

From Now On

Throughout this book we have looked at how the consciousness of humankind has evolved and taken us to a place where we as a species are being asked to step into our true identities and live on Earth as fully conscious beings. In fact we are right in the middle of taking that step regardless of whether we believe we are ready or even whether we are aware that it is happening. Life as we have known it is changing on a moment-to-moment basis. Long-held beliefs and certainties have been eroded, and institutions on which we relied to take care of and guide us have been shown to not have our best interests at heart; similarly influential individuals, to whom we have given our allegiance and trust, have been found to have 'feet of clay'.

We are being asked to let go of the limiting beliefs that have held us captive for the last 26,000 years and begin to accept our own divinity. In doing that, we must begin to live our lives on Earth as divine, unlimited beings, fully conscious of our divine nature and all that entails. This means no longer accepting the limitations that we have subscribed to in order to conform to societal norms. These 'societal norms' which were regarded as a necessity to provide stability and cohesion within the various societies have in reality had a divisive effect on humanity, and emphasized differences as opposed to similarities.

This approach has kept us separate from each other and has divided humanity along race, creed, gender, age and wealth to name but a few. We have been lulled into a false sense of security from which has developed apathy and helplessness. In this state we have lost touch with many of the gifts that we came on this Earth with, not only for our own use, but for the benefit of all humankind and the planet on which we reside.

We have lost the awareness that we are divine beings and as such are unlimited in our ability to create a life of our own choosing, a life that reflects our unique gifts and talents. This was the life that we came on this Earth to experience, not the one that we currently reside in where it seems that we are governed by rules, regulations and institutions that are there for the benefit of a few, and not for the good of all. In the current upheaval, the bright light of awareness is shining in to the darkest recesses of all those individuals and institutions that would claim to be working for the good of all. Their practices and belief systems are being exposed for all to see, and individuals are becoming aware of all that is being carried out in their name.

Groups of like-minded people are coming together, and in a peaceful non-violent way, reminiscent of the peace movement in India led by Mahatma Gandhi, merely stating: 'This is not acceptable, we want things to change'. The Arab Spring Revolution which has extended through 18 Middle Eastern countries and irrevocably changed the political landscape of many of these countries and the Occupy Wall Street movements which occurred in 90 countries throughout the world are both examples of where large groups of people have come together without any specific designated leaders to stand up and be counted. They have responded to a desire within for change, a recognition that this is not how they want to live and that there is something better that can be created. We are gradually awakening to the fact that change is needed, disconcerting though it may be. We are aware that there has to be another way, that the structures which we are currently employing are not working for the majority of people, and we are all being encouraged to ask: Where do we go from here? What else can we create? What else is possible?

We are in a new time, and trying to 'fix' systems and institutions using the same beliefs and processes from which they were created will not succeed for their time is past. We are not being asked to restore things to their former glory but are instead being guided to create new ones with core values that adhere to the rules of the Universe, and are inclusive of and for the betterment of all. It was Albert Einstein who remarked that only a fool looks for solutions in the same place that created the problem in the first instance.

Humankind is being shown that we are not master of all we survey. There is a greater power and a universal order that we are not only connected to, but are at one with. We are being made aware that every action we take affects everything, not only on this planet but in the Universe. We are part of a greater and grander plan that is now unfolding and are now being given a chance to consciously co-create with the Universe, to dream into reality a planet that is truly Heaven on Earth.

We have been equipped with all we require to make the changes; but we must become aware of what we have been given, and become competent in their use so that we may move seamlessly into the new world that is emerging. These gifts that we all enter into this world with have for eons been ignored, undervalued or sometimes regarded as downright dangerous and their use forbidden. We are being asked to reacquaint ourselves with these tools that we may use them first of all to empower ourselves, for we cannot help others to become aware of their own magnificence unless we first reveal our own.

There has been much written in the last few years on how to reclaim that divinity, for it appears 'awareness' on its own is not enough. We have developed so many 'bad habits' and limiting belief systems over thousands of years that it is not enough to say 'I am divine' and expect things to immediately fall into place. We are deeply imprinted right down to a DNA level with the cellular memories of not only our own lives, but those of our ancestors and our many past lives which influence and determine the lives that we will create.

A prerequisite of manifestation and actualization is that our subconscious beliefs must be in alignment with what we are trying to create if we are to be successful. They must hold the same vibrational energetic pattern as that which we are trying to attract. Given the many influences and dictates that we have absorbed over lifetimes it is not surprising that many of the beliefs that we hold are at variance with what we declare we desire. It might be wiser not to focus on manifesting what we think we want as often we discover that these objects bring us only temporary satisfaction; but rather focus on manifesting who we truly are. In this way we reclaim our birthright, and as divine beings are capable of actualizing all that we require for our time on this Earth.

The gap between Science and Spirituality is narrowing. The field of Quantum Physics has allowed objective measurement of many concepts which prior to this relied on faith for their existence. The scientific fact that everything on Earth including ourselves has its own energetic signature and vibrates at a measurable frequency has done much to redefine the concept of energy from a narrow, confined definition of 'conductor of force', to a more encompassing term which refers to its universal presence. The discovery of 'antimatter' has turned the Universe from a black space of emptiness and nothingness to an environment teeming with activity where an order exists that influences not only Earth but every planet, star and constellation in the galaxy. This has led to the questions, 'How did this order come to be here? Who designed and controls this order?' There is recognition that such a system did not develop by chance. This has led some quantum physicists to conclude that there is a presence, a greater intelligence at work that exists outside the parameters of humankind.

The year 2012 heralded the end of a planetary cycle in which the planets in our solar system adopted a particular alignment that has not occurred for the last 26,000 years and one which will not occur again for a further 26,000 years. The ancient peoples such as the Mayans who were also master astronomers could not see beyond this time and so their predictions and the now famous Mayan calendar stopped. It was not because they were predicting any great cataclysmic event, although some chose to interpret events in this manner and created a doomsday scenario that added to the fear and uncertainty that currently resides on the Earth at this time; but rather their experience and expertise did not allow them to plot with any further accuracy that which they did not have knowledge of.

How we view ourselves as a species is also changing on a variety of fronts. We as humans are being recognized not merely as biochemical bodies that are at the mercy of gravity and time, but as energetic beings whose thoughts, words, ideas and emotions create individual energetic patterns that affect the biochemistry of the body. The discovery of brain cells in heart tissue has given rise to the hypothesis that the heart actually receives sensory information before the brain, and that decisions are made at the heart level prior to the brain beginning the process of sensory integration and logical analysis. This 'intuitive intelligence' is becoming recognized as a valid form of intelligence in its own right similar to the cognitive or emotional intelligence already identified. The importance of intuitive intelligence is beginning to be realized as it now provides a measure of what hitherto was known as intuition and was dismissed as unimportant as it could not be scientifically measured.

These disclosures are influencing the direction of modern medicine and initiating new interest and research in the possible use of 'energy' as a 'medicine' and providing a viable alternative to pharmaceuticals. The research that has identified the power of thoughts, words and prayers in healing the body has also highlighted that we are less victims of genetics and body variances than we have been led to believe, and have a more active role in creating good health that we realize. Our own thoughts, ideas, familial and emotional beliefs hold the key not only to the level of health we create but also the lifestyle that we ultimately live. This of course changes everything and places a greater responsibility on the individual to create wisely, as the choices we make have a direct impact on the quality of life and health that we will have.

We, as human beings, need connection with our fellow human beings and traditionally this was provided by the family and its place within the community. Mass migration, immigration, and displacement whether voluntary such as for economic reasons or involuntary as a result of wars, natural disasters, or forced repatriation have served to break the strong bonds of family and community, resulting in the emergence of new societies and communities unlimited by distance, time or space.

The nature and duration of our personal relationships are also changing and we no longer can rely on the familiar familial structure of the nuclear family as a blueprint for family life. Many relationships are of a much shorter duration than previously, and it is wholly probable that an adult will have more than one serious relationship and may indeed be parent to a number of children with a number of different partners. The modern family is much more diverse than before, and the individuals within that family exposed to many more ideas and conflicting belief systems. It can also mean that there may be difficulties in finding where they belong in society and to what belief system or group they align with. This has caused many young people to look outside family groupings for their sense of identity and allegiance, and contributed in some areas to the development of gangs and the gang culture, with belief systems that operate outside accepted norms and which wreak so much havoc and destruction on the communities in which they occur.

On a more global level the emergence of social networks via the Internet has allowed massive numbers of like-minded people to be drawn together with the intent of communicating and being part of an electronically-based society. At present the physical and electronic communities exist side by side with the majority of people having a foot in both camps. However, there are those who exist exclusively in one camp with only brief forays in to the other, and then there is a further group unconnected to either. Many of these individuals feeling lost or alone, unaligned to any particular grouping; in occupying this place their feelings of separation grow and are fed by their own thoughts and fears. These marginalized people operating on the fringes of accepted society remain unaware of their own magnificence and creative ability intent as they are on basic day-to-day survival.

It has been argued that society, as we have known it, is breaking down and that all the social ills which we are experiencing are as a result of this breakdown. An alternative viewpoint is that society is not so much breaking down as 'breaking through', which while appearing chaotic at the moment offers the opportunity to create a society that is aligned with the new values currently being birthed here on Earth. The society which is emerging has the potential to be globally inclusive with a place for and acceptance of all. This will necessitate the suspension of judgment and the development of discernment and intuition so that while each individual would have the opportunity to display their uniqueness, those viewing it would use their intuitive intelligence to determine if it was appropriate for them or not.

This is one of the current difficulties with the Internet or electronic community, where lack of discernment means that many of those viewing information have no idea of its accuracy or intent. As we further develop discernment it transforms into an innate knowing, which is the emergence of intuition and the third aspect in this trilogy is trust in our discernment and intuition. In this way is wisdom developed and we move from being collectors of information to receptacles of knowledge, which we can use to guide us in creating the life we wish to experience and avoiding the pitfalls and traps which can befall the unaware.

One of the most disquieting aspects of all the global changes we have encountered to date – whether it be in weather patterns, the banking crisis, economic recession, the changes in our personal circumstances, or relationships – is that increased level of uncertainty that we have had to accommodate and integrate. As humans we like to have certainty; this is obvious in all aspects of life but never more so when it comes to having monetary wealth. If people are asked why they want to be rich rarely do they reply that it is for the love of money, but rather it is the certainty that it brings and the illusion of control that it engenders.

The certainty that objects or items can be purchased when desired, that the future is taken care of, that there is choice on the lifestyle that can be lived and that it is there if needed in any case of emergency. It is the sense of security or certainty that it brings and the freedom from worry. This is why most people desire wealth. The same can be said of saving money: the certainty that if a financial emergency occurs the resources are there to deal with it; likewise going for an annual medical check-up (to be certain there is nothing wrong), insurance of all kinds whether it be medical, house, car, life – with all these we are trying to buy certainty that if anything untoward happens then the solution is there, the resources are there.

In this new world that is in the process of being birthed, where certainty is not there we are being asked to trust in uncertainty and to be comfortable in not knowing. This goes against all our core beliefs. We have been taught all our lives to prepare for the rainy day, to think ahead; in fact our basic survival has always been based on our ability to infer, deduct and predict. The money markets currently operate on these tenets, as do all insurance companies and financial institutions.

Our modern lives are predicated on these abilities, and yet if we examine the major events that have occurred in any field, whether financial, personal, political, economic or social, all have been affected by situations that no one predicted occurring. The sense of shock and disbelief following these incidents rippled down throughout society affecting many individuals and families, forcing them to reconsider their future plans and the directions their lives were to take. A prime example was the collapse of the Lehman Brothers financial institution in 2008, triggering not only a massive worldwide crisis in the financial industry; but on a social and personal level was the catalyst for unemployment in many sectors.

This has had a devastating effect on many individuals and families causing them to reevaluate the ways in which they lived their lives and what they considered priorities. Dramatic changes ensued and while many took the opportunity to change the course and direction of their lives entirely, others tried and some are still trying desperately to recreate what has been lost. Homes have been repossessed, and many have had their sense of identity altered by the circumstances in which they have found themselves, particularly if that identity revolved around the job that they did or the home or items that they possessed.

In such instances it is very easy to allow the ego to take over and declare that all is lost, that the individual is worthless and a nothing, and their life hopeless. It takes courage, bravery and determination to carry on in the face of such adversity yet it is in these very conditions that it is all to play for. It has been noted in the past that many more millionaires are created in times of perceived recession than in periods of perceived economic stability. There is an opportunity being presented to create the lives that the soul yearns for, a life that was dreamt about but was dismissed because it was not deemed possible, or thought to be financially viable.

It has been estimated that approximately 90% of those who have been made unemployed were in jobs that they did not enjoy, or find fulfilling. They did them because they needed the money or they could not think of anything else to do. They drifted into them and stayed believing they were capable of nothing else and finding comfort in the familiarity, or becoming trapped in the need to financially provide for themselves and others.

People are now being encouraged to live a life that is meaningful and fulfilling to them, or at least become aware that they have choice and to start asking how they can achieve this. They are being guided to relinquish and adjust the beliefs that they hold about life and how it must be a struggle in order to succeed; in fact in some sections of society success without struggle is almost seen as worthless. There is a belief that working hard is the only way to ensure success and while it is true that action is still necessary in order to create it, it no longer needs to be the 24 hour all-consuming endurance marathon that previously had been cited as the recipe to success.

In such a gargantuan struggle to achieve success which has often equated to financial abundance and power within a company or corporation, families were lost, health compromised, integrity sacrificed and a form of economic slavery embarked upon. In the new corporate world which is still being fashioned, corporate greed and corruption will no longer be tolerated or permitted. Transparency, honesty, moral and ethical governance will become the norm in all business transactions whether big or small. It will not be a case of the harder you work the greater your success or indeed who you know that will determine the outcome of your endeavors, but rather the extent to which you are in tune, and in the flow of the creative energy that flows through and governs the economic development of life on Earth.

If in the flow, you will create with apparent ease and little effort as you will always be in the right place at the right time, and you will be using intuition, discernment and trust to take the action necessary to guarantee success. It is the difference between paddling downstream using the river current for energy while you put your focus on steering in the direction you wish to go and avoiding all obstacles that you may encounter versus paddling upstream against the current where the greatest effort and focus is on moving forward and mastering the current, never mind noticing oncoming dangers and obstacles. Which sounds like more fun? Which leaves you energy to enjoy life as opposed to being drained by it?

It would seem we are being given little option but to change, and how we approach and integrate that change is very much our decision. We can fight and rail against it tooth and nail, or view it as a rare and precious opportunity to make a difference and take part in the creation of a new society which reflects the next stage in the evolution of humanity, sure in the knowledge that within us we have all the tools necessary to successfully achieve that task, and in the process create a life and a world of peace that we can truly be proud of and joyful in. To achieve this we are being asked to step fully into our power by accepting firstly that we are infinite beings and that as such we are capable of creating whatever we decide we want to create. In fact we are unconsciously creating all the time, and if we wish to see what we have created, look at the life that you are living for that is your creation.

There are parts that we like and then there are parts that we would like to change; those aspects which we would like to change are usually where we are living a lie or where we have sold ourselves short in order to fit in with another's version of how things should be. We have bought the lie that you can't do this or you can't have that, or that it has to be this way. We are living someone else's version or reality and it doesn't feel 'right' to us. We have an inner knowing when something is the truth or when we are not being told the whole truth. The lie may not be deliberate, but may reflect the limited beliefs of another; but we can no longer be less than we truly are. This means moving past limitations and using intuition, trust and discernment to guide us along the path. We are being actively encouraged in this environment of free will to express thoughts and ideas which empower us into being.

We came on this Earth to experience life, to live fully in the moment, safe in the knowledge that we have within us all the talents and abilities that we need for a joyful, abundant life on Earth; but over the ages those talents and abilities have become hidden in the general fear, panic and helplessness that has developed. Now is the time to reacquaint ourselves with our own magnificence and to accept nothing less than absolutely everything as our divine birthright. This is an abundant Universe that does not know the meaning of lack, but we have been duped into believing that there is scarcity and as a result have forgotten how to receive fully that which the Divine Creative Force freely and abundantly gives. In reestablishing our relationship with the Divine Creative Force we are opening ourselves to the knowing that our requests will be fulfilled unreservedly, that there is no need to implore or beg, that as Divine beings we are co-creators with the Divine Creative Force and from that space we can bring into the physical realm that which we wish to create.

There are certain caveats in the process of manifestation that are required if the process is to be successful. The most important is that we have to be vibrationally compatible with what we are trying to attract and create. In other words our individual vibrational signature must oscillate at a similar frequency to that which we want to have in our lives. Our vibrational signature is unique to us and is made up of the beliefs, thoughts, ideas and emotions which we broadcast into the Universe on a moment-by-moment basis.

Once vibrationally compatible we must also recognize that there is an element of 'Divine Timing' inherent in the process. On Earth we really only view a small piece of what is a very big picture. Our belief in and referencing of linear time as the only measure of movement within the time-space continuum limits our awareness of happenings on a more universal level and so while at the more conscious level the mind may desire instant manifestation of what we have requested, there is an aspect of us referred to as the Higher Self or Soul that will wait for the optimum moment to deliver what has been requested in a way that is best suited to the individual and in a manner that will facilitate best that which the soul wishes to experience. An awareness of this allows for the development of trust and faith in the process of manifestation and an understanding that the delivery of those requests into the physical dimension may occur differently from our imaginings, but will occur in a way that will be much more than we ever asked for, because unlike us the Divine Creative Force has no limitations.

The energy of consciousness is being beamed constantly on to the Earth plane at this time and it brings with it new understandings almost on a daily basis. It is also reactivating within each of us an awareness of the concept of 'oneness'. The idea that we are all connected and interconnected on an energetic level not only with our fellow humans that inhabit the Earth plane but with every living species, be it animal, plant, rock or mineral on this planet. We are conjoined in an energetic matrix that spans the length and breadth of this planet and holds all within its care, so that a butterfly flapping its wings in Japan can effect a change in the tides in California.

The ancient peoples recognized this and that was why they saw themselves as guardians or custodians of Gaia or the Earth. They viewed their actions as having a direct impact on the wellbeing of Mother Earth and so took no more than they needed for their own survival, ever mindful of the gifts they were being given. There was an awareness that their survival depended on the health and well-being of Mother Earth and all the species contained within. They did not see themselves as superior to the other species on Earth nor did they view the other species as inferior. They recognized that the plant forms provided food and medicines, that the animal species provided meat and materials for clothing, that the forests and rocks provided building materials, and the rivers provided water which was the elixir of survival.

They recognized that there was an energetic balance among 'All', what we now refer to as an ecosystem, and that if this was disturbed or broken would have dire consequences for all Earth's inhabitants. This energetic matrix has now been identified by quantum physicists and its properties are being uncovered in ways that indicate that the beliefs of many of the indigenous peoples of the world hold within them more than a grain of truth. The Aborigines of Australia when they went walkabout in the outback could find water by 'singing' it to them. Were they really describing an ability of being aware of the vibration of water which allowed them to follow the energy to its source? Were many of the skills that the local medicine men were revered for more to do with being vibrationally aware as opposed to 'magic'?

The terms 'vibrational energy' and 'vibrational compatibility' were not around in times past, and so the indigenous people tended to speak and use language that reflected their daily lives and experiences. That concept of oneness is being resurrected again that we might truly remember where we came from and what we have come on this Earth both to experience and reestablish; as much as we are reopening dialogue with the Divine Creative Force so too are we reestablishing a dialogue with Mother Earth and asking her what we can give her rather than what she will give to us.

There never has been a period when humanity is being given so much help and opportunity to remove itself from the apathetic, limited and helpless state that is accepted as life here on Earth. We are being awakened to the magnificence of our own being and given insight to the divinity that lies within and what is possible with awareness and mastery of the inherent talents and abilities. In addition the chains of limitations and limited beliefs are being removed one after the other.

We are being presented with the opportunity to create the life that we always knew was possible, but believed that we could not have because we were not good enough, valuable enough, perfect enough etc. Essentially we were programmed to believe what could not be achieved. Now we have the awareness that as divine beings we are capable of creating anything that we choose effortlessly in tune with the Divine Creative Force, and that all we have to do is choose and then be willing to receive and accept that which we have asked for. It is as simple as that.

The past thousands of years have been spent emphasizing our humanity and the frailty of that humanity. It was taught that what separated man from the beasts was his soul, but for many it was something separate and remote from daily life. It only appeared on high days and holidays for a brief period and then was forgotten about. It was nothing to do with daily living, never acknowledged, or known, spoken about in reverent tones and generally ignored. In fact for many it was not seen as an aspect of the self, rather something outside of it.

Now the time has come to reestablish a relationship and dialogue with that aspect of self that is divine, and invite it back into our lives to offer wisdom, guidance and a direct connection to the Divine Creative Force. We are not alone or helpless; we are divine beings having a human experience. There is nothing wrong with us, there was never anything wrong with us; we merely need to recognize our own magnificence and believe in our own divinity and in that knowing dare to step into our full power to create the life that we came on Earth to live.

Acknowledgments

My heartfelt thanks to everyone who had a part in the writing of this book, for their ongoing help, guidance and support.

To Barbara Meiklejohn-Free for her kindness and encouragement in providing a vital step in this book's journey.

To the wonderful Kate Osborne, Solarus Ltd, for her wise counsel, expertise, patience and skill in the editing of this book.

About the Author

Lucy O'Hagan is native to Northern Ireland, undertaking her first Degree in Psychology and Linguistics (Human Communication) in Belfast before completing her studies in Clinical Communication Studies in London, England. She has worked as a practitioner in the National Health Service in both the UK and Northern Ireland where she practiced as a Paediatric Clinical Specialist Speech & Language Therapist before moving to Co. Wicklow in Ireland to take up a senior post with the Health Services Executive.

Her interest in Clinical Research saw her take part in a joint research project with the Speech & Language Therapy Department at Galway University and resulted in a paper being published in the American Journal of Audiology 2011. She has travelled extensively and visited many of the sacred and ancient sites throughout the world. Lucy's interest in Esoteric Healing and Eastern Philosophy has continued parallel to her career in Allopathic therapies, and saw her study both in India and China where she completed her training in Traditional Chinese Medicine at Nanjing University, Nanjing, China specializing in Acupuncture.

She has also added many healing modalities to her repertoire over the years including Medical Massage and Reiki. Her work over the years has afforded her a unique opportunity to gain theoretical and practical knowledge in both Western and Eastern healing modalities, and by drawing on these diverse perspectives the traditional and the modern have been brought together in a fusion that has culminated in the content of this book.

BOOKS

O is a symbol of the world, of oneness and unity. In different cultures it also means the "eye," symbolizing knowledge and insight. We aim to publish books that are accessible, constructive and that challenge accepted opinion, both that of academia and the "moral majority."

Our books are available in all good English language bookstores worldwide. If you don't see the book on the shelves ask the bookstore to order it for you, quoting the ISBN number and title. Alternatively you can order online (all major online retail sites carry our titles) or contact the distributor in the relevant country, listed on the copyright page.

See our website www.o-books.net for a full list of over 500 titles, growing by 100 a year.

And tune in to myspiritradio.com for our book review radio show, hosted by June-Elleni Laine, where you can listen to the authors discussing their books.

MySpiritRadio